THE INCARCERATION OF
NATIVE AMERICAN WOMEN

**New Visions in Native American
and Indigenous Studies**

SERIES EDITORS

Margaret D. Jacobs
Robert J. Miller

The Incarceration of Native American Women

Creating Pathways to Wellness and
Recovery through Gentle Action Theory

Carma Corcoran

CO-PUBLISHED BY THE UNIVERSITY OF NEBRASKA PRESS

AND THE AMERICAN PHILOSOPHICAL SOCIETY

Library of Congress Control Number: 2022051942

Set in Charis by Mikala R. Kolander.

CONTENTS

TABLES

My interest in the issue of incarceration grew out of my lived experience as a Native American person. I come from a significantly large family, and from my early childhood I can remember three things distinctly when it comes to my awareness of incarceration. First, that I did not like it when a patrol car with a uniformed officer of the law pulled up in front of where we were living; second, that my mother hated law enforcement; and third, that one or more of my brothers would be "away." I missed my brothers and I worried about them. As it turned out, the last time I saw some of my older brothers they were being taken "away," and as a result of my family imploding, I would never see or speak to them again, at least not in this physical world.

As a young woman living in an adopted family, I was part of an ecumenical youth group led by my adopted parents. We performed in a wide variety of venues ranging from churches in the area to retirement homes and a couple of juvenile and prison facilities. These performances included drama, music, and dance. I must truthfully note that I have zero talent in any of these areas, but I was living in a talented fine arts family, and I suppose they thought I might get some talent via osmosis.

The trips to the juvenile halls and prisons were particularly meaningful for me. I would always see prisoners that I could tell were Native American. I could tell that they knew I was Native American. We would eye each other with an unspoken understanding of our connection to each other. We would exchange the Native nod, which is subtle and often accompanied by a shy smile fostering an understanding of our relationship as Native people. In these places I would look deeply into the captive audiences, wondering if any of these Native prisoners were my brothers, my uncles, my aunties, my cousins, my nephews, or my nieces. I wondered and worried about how long they were "in" for and how they were faring. I wanted to talk to them. I wanted to find out where they were from. Perhaps they were from my tribe or my reservation. But of course, that kind of interaction wasn't allowed. My feelings were ones of sadness, loneliness, and yet I hoped by my being there, smiling and singing for them, that in some way this helped them. These were not thoughts and feelings that I shared with anyone until I was an adult and then only with a select few.

Upon being removed from my family, I was sent to a foster home. Unlike many children, Native and non-Native, I had a safe, loving, and wonderful foster family and home. I was even able to have a couple play dates with two of my brothers, which I remember to this day. After eighteen months in my foster home, I was adopted. My birth family never left my heart, soul, and mind. I was fortunate to have a continued relationship with my foster father and mother. I would visit them for a week each summer until just before I graduated from high school. They lived near my reservation in Montana, Rocky Boy's Indian Reservation. As we would travel back and forth from their home to the border town of Havre, Montana, we would pass the marked turnoff to the reservation. I always wanted to ask them to take me there, and I know they would have if I could have uttered my request. But something kept me back. When we were in town doing errands, I would subtly investigate the faces of the Native people we encountered and wonder who they were and if they knew on some level who I was. My foster mother kindly kept me up on family news. She would send me newspaper clippings of births, arrests, and deaths. I was often mentioned in the obituaries even though I had been away for years. I knew I was not forgotten. In my twenties I was able to reconnect with my family members who still lived on or near our reservation. It was life-changing, and I would take my first trip "home" for the wake of one of my brothers. In my thirties I reconnected with my youngest living siblings, who are twins, and one of whom is my only sister. I know how fortunate I am to have "found" my family.

As I matured into adulthood and sought meaningful work in all aspects of my life—personal, academic, and professional—my concentration became centered on issues important to Native American people. Creator brought me the opportunity to volunteer in the women's prison here where I live in Oregon. The experience of going inside the prison showed me where my focus needed to be in my academic and social justice work. I accepted that I was not going to move back to Montana, but I wanted to serve my family, my tribe, and my people in some way. I wanted to serve incarcerated Native people because of my brothers, nieces, and nephews, and for my own hurting heart. As I gained more cultural knowledge, I understood that while I wanted to serve on behalf of my brothers, there were many areas where that would not be culturally appropriate for me as a Native woman. It is from that place in the journey of addressing the societal issue of incarceration of Native American women—its causality, the ancillary affects, the need for healing, and the methodology of providing healing practices—that my trajectory brought me to writing this book.

ACKNOWLEDGMENTS

It is impossible to complete the journey from a dissertation to a writing a book without a circle of support. I first need to thank and give honor to Creator and the Ancestors. There is a Native American saying that is appropriate to share here: "Every step you take is supported by a thousand ancestors." I have felt their love, support, redirection, and pride. This has been a journey of ceremony that I have held before Creator and the Ancestors daily. Creator and the Ancestors have blessed my efforts to do this research in a "good way" by providing me avenues to tribal experts, my Elders, and authors who are distinguished, credible, and authentic.

My dissertation committee of the late F. David Peat, PhD, Michael A. Raffanti, EdD, and Mary Clare, PhD, provided their expertise, guidance, and valuable suggestions to me. I express my deepest thanks and gratitude for their support. The issues that are core to my research could not have been addressed in the way I wanted to write without the seminal work of three incredible authors. The theory of gentle action created by F. David Peat melded with my preferred way of being in the world while providing me the needed theory to contrast and discuss traditional ways of knowing and being for Native American people. Shawn Wilson, PhD (Opaskwayak Cree), provided the template I needed to form my dissertation while emphasizing the concept that research is ceremony and that as a Native American researcher, it is imperative that I do the work in a good way. The work of Luana Ross, PhD (Confederated Salish and Kootenai Tribes), provided the foundational knowledge, written from the Native American perspective of the experience of incarcerated Native American women. Thank you to each of you for your life-changing work. My hands are up and my spirit is grateful.

Without Shari Lachin's hard work, heart, and trustworthiness, my dissertation and book proposal could not have been completed. Thank you to Meghan Krausch, PhD, for their work copyediting, and to Meghsha Sqawsan Barner for their research work. Thank you to my friend Amy Frank Meabe for her editing and feedback. A heartfelt thank you to Frank Pommersheim for his immeasurable feedback, support, and friendship. Thank you to my publisher, the University of Nebraska Press, and to editors Matt Bokovoy and Heather Stauffer. Thank you to Robert J. Miller for his support.

Being so far away from home I do not have access to my Elders except for the few times when I am able to travel to Rocky Boy. Here in Portland I have been blessed with a group of Native American women who have graciously formed a circle of support for me. They support me spiritually, culturally, and in my academic pursuits while sharing their wisdom with me. Ruth Jensen (Lingit, a.k.a Tlingit), Celeste Whitewolf, JD (Confederated Tribes of the Umatilla Indians), Jill Shepherd, MA (Santee Sioux of Nebraska and Eyak village, Alaska), Elaine St. Martin (Tuscarora/Seneca), Louise Seymour Wilmes (Native Hawaiian / Otoe-Missouria Tribe of Oklahoma), and Mary Elaine Priester have encouraged me, offered me their wisdom, and deepened our relationships individually and as a group. My hands are up in gratitude to every one of them.

Employing an Indigenous research paradigm requires ethical components discussed in the dissertation. Holding myself accountable to my Elders and my people has been central to the research ceremony. I took two trips home to Rocky Boy over the last year. Thank you to my family members, my sister-in-law Margaret Bernard (Chippewa Cree), and my nieces Misty Denny (Chippewa Cree) and Melody Whitford (Chippewa Cree), whose hospitality, assistance, and support allowed me to do research and spend time with them. They answered my questions about family, culture, and our tribe. Through their efforts of fostering connection, I was able to meet and spend time with a group of my women Elders.

These Elders are well respected in our tribe and are keepers of knowledge and medicine. My hands are up and my heart is full as I give thanks to five Chippewa Cree Elders who enriched my course and smoothed the way: Pearl Raining Bird Whitford, Pauline Standing Rock, Frances Top Sky, Helen Parker, and Luanne Belcourt. Spending time with them, their willingness to answer my questions, and their good wishes and prayers have provided me a connection to my tribe, the Cree culture, and family, all of which my soul needed. My godfather Earl Arkinson (Chippewa Cree) held me up in prayer and gifted me my Native American adult name.

Thank you to my circle of association. From school friends spanning grade school and beyond I have had countless people sending me encouraging words and their support. The Native American community here in Portland and throughout the country has held me up in prayer, validated my work, and been enthusiastic about my dream. Thank you to those who presented in the Healing the Sacred Hoop workshop that I led using gentle action theory.

The most profound thanks go to the circle of women who formed the Healing the Sacred Hoop workshop at Coffee Creek Correctional Institution. You brought heart and life to the ideas that had been ruminating in my heart and mind. Thank you to the women I have mentored. Your trust and faith and your allowing me into your lives is one of the greatest gifts of my lifetime. Please remember that this work is for you, it is about you, it is about your families, it is about our families. It is about your ancestors. It is about my ancestors. It is about our people. It is about healing and the journey home.

I have an incredibly large extended family. I have a birth family, a foster family, an adoptive family, a family by marriage, and the family my husband and I created together. I must thank my family. My daughter, Kari Beller, has made my life's journey complete with the gift of being her mother. Welcoming our son-in-law, Rodney Beller, into our lives as a husband and father has expanded our little family. Together Kari and Rodney have given us the greatest joy of our lives, our grandson, Jaron Beller. Jaron has increased the capacity of our hearts to love far beyond what we ever knew was possible. Jaron and I have a bond that is so deep and true, and I am blessed beyond words having his love and support. Last, and not the least, is my husband, Don Corcoran.

THE INCARCERATION OF
NATIVE AMERICAN WOMEN

CHAPTER 1

Native American Women and Incarceration

INCARCERATION AS A SOCIETAL ISSUE

MYRNA—TSALAGI (CHEROKEE)

I first met Myrna when she was incarcerated at the Coffee Creek Correctional Facility located south of Portland, Oregon. I had begun going into the prison as a support volunteer under the umbrella of the Religious Services of the Oregon Department of Corrections. I was fortunate to get to know her in the last two years of her incarceration and have an ongoing friendship with her today.

Myrna was in her late forties when we first met. She has generously allowed me to share some of her story. She was widowed in her early forties and was raising her grandchildren when she received some shattering news about her health. She was told to get her affairs in order. She had been struggling emotionally and financially since the death of her husband and was unable to cope with the news, sharing that she did not have the tools to cope with the pain. With what seemed to her like the final blow, Myrna went on a two-week drunk. Her drunk ended when she hit a person while driving intoxicated.

Myrna was arrested and lodged in the Benton County jail in Corvallis, Oregon. She was in jail for six months before her family was able to come up with the funds to bail her out. Her attorney, who was a public defender, wanted her to take a plea deal. Myrna refused because the charges included one for being under the influence of drugs. She had never done drugs and did not want to plead to a charge that was false. Her attorney said she was facing fifty-seven years in prison with two charges: assault with a deadly weapon (the car) and drunk driving.

Myrna ran. She took off for Alabama, where she knew someone, and was on the run for ten months. She had made one telephone call, a call to her mother in Oregon. She and her friend were getting ready to leave for Louisiana because she was feeling as though she was being watched. The day before the trip to Louisiana, the house was surrounded and entered by a SWAT team. The run was over. The extradition process to Oregon began.

It would take forty days for Myrna to get back to Oregon. She was delivered first to Georgia and then transported via the Justice Prisoner and Alien Transportation System (JPATS), nicknamed "Con Air," to Oklahoma. Upon her arrival, shackled, at the facility in Oklahoma City, the airplane transporting her landed and pulled into the inside of prison; it was an eerie experience for her as the giant hangar doors closed, delivering her into the dark and massive bowels of the prison.

Myrna had gotten her period on the flight. Being shackled, she had no means of stopping the blood from flowing all over her and the seat. Not being able to take care of her needs, she recalls feeling like an animal. Upon her arrival in Oregon, she obtained a new public defender whom she really liked and who listened to her. She received a thirty-six-month prison sentence with an additional ten months for absconding. The judge originally gave her credit for time served, which would have erased the extra ten months. However, days before she thought she was going home, she was informed that the Department of Corrections would not honor the credit for time served given by the judge. She would serve the extra ten months. We will circle back to Myrna's story later.

Incarceration is a societal issue for Native Americans. Incarceration statistics are alarmingly high for Native Americans, including men, women, and youth. Jamaal Bell (2010) contends that not only are Native Americans ignored in the discussions of mass incarceration and racial disparities—they are in fact highly overrepresented in the criminal justice system as an ethnic minority. The incarceration of Native Americans is 38 percent higher than the national rate, with law enforcement agents arresting American Indians and Alaska Natives at twice the rate of the greater U.S. population, and on average Native people are sentenced to longer terms than non-Indians for crimes related to property and violence. Suicide is a problem not only outside the prison walls but inside as well, with suicide rates for American Native inmates higher than for non-Indians. Unfortunately, according to Bell, there are few statistical reports specifically addressing the incarceration rates of Native American women, which reflects the lack of care and interest for our women.

Incarceration runs deeply through my family. Living and working in Oregon, far away from my family in Montana, I wondered about Native American men and women incarcerated in Oregon. I began to do some research about the prison system in Oregon. At the same time, I was beginning work on my PhD and exploring the intersection of *gentle action theory* and *traditional ways* in the provision of service to Native Americans affected by incarceration. While my concentration was centered on Montana and Oregon, I was also able to gather information from other parts of the United States, which demonstrates the need to address this societal issue. Additionally, I am an enrolled member of the Chippewa Cree Nation with my lineage being predominantly Cree, and therefore I have done some research looking at the experience of the First Nations people of Canada. There are similar issues and outcomes when looking at systems, socioeconomic status, historical trauma, and racism with the same need for hope, healing, and access to culturally specific services for all Indigenous people.

The Oregon Department of Corrections (ODOC) does not provide accurate statistics regarding the number of Native women incarcerated at the Coffee Creek Correctional Facility (CCCF), the only prison for women in the state of Oregon, because the intake process does not include a question on ethnicity. Intake staff use two methods to determine race: They make assumptions based on an inmate's last name and physical characteristics. If an incoming inmate speaks out about her ethnicity during the intake process, there is an additional chance that it will be noted in her file.

While working at a nonprofit, directing a program that sought to provide mentors for children who had one parent or both in prison, I attended a conference on juvenile justice held on the Umatilla Indian Reservation. During lunchtime, attendees were given the opportunity to share information. A woman stood up and spoke about how volunteers were needed to go into CCCF to assist with spiritual services. I introduced myself to the woman and expressed an interest in volunteering. Red Lodge volunteers serve under the Religious Services umbrella at the prison. I ended up being a Red Lodge volunteer and eventually the board chair for several years.

RED LODGE TRANSITION SERVICES

Red Lodge Transition Services in Oregon is a much-needed program. According to their website,

> Red Lodge Transition Services is a non-profit grass roots organization supported by volunteers who have experience working with men and women in prison. Our primary objective is to assist Native men and women who are ready to transition from prison, jail, and treatment back to community. Creating a realistic plan for transition can be very stressful! There are many obstacles and barriers each person, family and community must navigate through in order to be successful. Red Lodge Transition Services is working to identify barriers and help prepare people for successful re-entry.

SUCCESSFUL TRANSITION

Successful transition depends on meeting spiritual, mental, emotional and physical needs. It is a complex process which takes place between the individual, family and community. Major emotional, spiritual and physical adjustments are made within the first thirty days of re-entry. How is it possible for positive change to occur when basic survivor needs such as housing, employment, legal identification, transportation, food and emotional support are not available? There are many elements associated with creating and sustaining a successful transition program. (Red Lodge Transition Services, n.d.)

Red Lodge is a unique program in many ways. Volunteers begin working with Native American women while they are incarcerated at CCCF by providing spiritual services. Spiritual services include talking circle, sweat, smudging, and the First Foods Feast. In addition, a variety of workshops have been offered, such as "Healing the Sacred Hoop," "Know Your Rights," and "Positive Indian Parenting." Red Lodge brings in Elders, spiritual leaders, and community members throughout all their program services. The majority of the volunteers are Native American. Many of the Red Lodge board members, past and present, have been incarcerated.

The essential component of Red Lodge's work with the women is providing connection to culture, access to community, and spiritual teaching and ceremony. The women served by the program have been sentenced to anywhere from three years to life in prison. Some women have been involved with the criminal justice system since they were underage. Red Lodge volunteers are in the prison on a consistent basis, allowing the opportunity to build relationships, trust, and respect, which creates a pathway to healing. Red Lodge is the principal resource for the women as they plan their reentry to community.

Red Lodge seeks to assist women in their transition out of prison. They are a source of referral for a myriad of social service needs, including housing, food, clothing, transportation, and Native American substance abuse programs. Red Lodge hopes to help the women find a pathway to community by connecting the women to Native American cultural groups in the Portland area. Not all women are paroling out to the Portland area. For those women outside the area, Red Lodge attempts to connect them to services in the area where they will be paroled. Women who parole out to Portland and the surrounding area are sometimes connected to a mentor, either in the community or someone with whom they can be in contact with via telephone, text, social media, and email. I have mentored a number of women. There is no designated termination of the mentoring relationship or the relationship between the women and me, because it is the "Native Way" to develop ties for a lifetime and not to withdraw your support. When listening to Red Lodge volunteers discuss incarceration, one will always hear, "Culture is the answer." Having worked with the women in prison and having relationships with women in my circle of mentoring, I have been fortunate to apply gentle action theory in my work and activism.

As the former board chair of Red Lodge, I worked with many other community members volunteering in the Religious Services program at CCCF. Red Lodge continues to provide spiritual services in both minimum and medium security units. In 2013, as I prepared to conduct the Healing the Sacred Hoop workshop series, a survey was conducted by Red Lodge to determine how many Native American women were in CCCF at that time. While we were not able to poll 100 percent of the women in CCCF, inmates attending the spiritual program were polled. As of March 1, 2015, the Oregon Department of Corrections Inmate Population Profile listed 21 women as American Indian out of an inmate population of 643 (ODOC 2015, 1). The Red Lodge poll determined that 50 Native women in medium-security and 75 in minimum-security units were being served. The ODOC number is grossly inaccurate; Red Lodge, which continues to provide spiritual services at CCCF as well as to poll participants, estimates a minimum of 150 Native women incarcerated at CCCF. In addition, ODOC does not provide a breakdown as to tribal affiliation for the women who are counted as Native American. As a result of this inaccuracy, I included in my research the other place I call home, the state of Montana, to supplement the information missing from the Oregon data. I am from Montana, the bulk of my family lives in Montana, and many of my relatives cycle in and out of incarceration in the state of Montana. Concentrating on the places I call home, both Montana and Oregon, has allowed me to remain authentic both in the research process and in its practical application.

While facilitating the Healing the Sacred Hoop workshop inside the prison, there were opportunities and challenges. The greatest opportunity was that I got to put on the workshop and that I was able to use gentle action theory as the method. I believe that the workshop was allowed for three reasons: Red Lodge volunteers had been providing spiritual services for many years; CCCF had determined that the original twelve participants were "incorrigible"; if we failed, the ODOC could contend that they had at least let us "try."

There were also challenges working within a prison, the top three being: (1) The women could be pulled from the group if they had an infraction, resulting in the possibility of missing a session or, worst-case scenario, being sent to segregation. (2) We were on a strict two-hour time limit each week, and if we ran over the allotted time, the women would have to check in to their cells late, which could result in an infraction. (3) We had to follow all the rules of the institution and had to make sure that the women were not breaking any physical contact rules. This meant while they could, under our watch, give a quick reassuring hug to a group member, they could not sit thigh-to-thigh, hold hands, or kiss each other.

These opportunities and challenges were good for me because they allowed me to be thankful for the opportunities and inspired me to deal with the challenges. The workshop continues to be held, but those conducting it do not use gentle action theory. Conducting the workshop using gentle action theory provided an opportunity both to do research and to apply the theory.

Learning more about incarceration as a societal issue prompted research about the criminal justice system in the state of Montana. It was during this process that I was first exposed to the work of Luana Ross.

THE MONTANA EXPERIENCE

Ross (1998) has written the most comprehensive book to date about the experience of Native American women who are incarcerated. Ross is an enrolled member of the Confederated Salish and Kootenai Tribes and grew up on the Flathead Indian Reservation in Montana. She grew up across the street from the tribal jail, and she could see prisoners walking around and visiting. The jail was seldom locked. In comparison, her experience mirrors that of many of us, as Native Americans, having relatives cycle in and out of prison. She speaks of being a child and feeling as if people appeared to vanish and magically reappear, going away and returning from imprisonment. I can recall being a small child on Rocky Boy's Indian Reservation in Montana and missing my brothers, who cycled in and out of the juvenile justice system on work farms. At first I understood them to be "over in Miles City," and as I grew older, I came to know what that meant, that my three oldest brothers were incarcerated.

Ross (1998) provides a historical context in which Native Americans began to be identified and categorized as criminals. She outlines the history of Native-white relations in Montana, which is one of racism and oppression. She addresses the concept of sovereignty, describing it as "a fragile concept whose meaning is shaped and reshaped by legislation and court decisions" (Ross 1998, 3). She asserts that Native American criminality is inexorably tied, in a complex and historical way, to the loss of sovereignty, which began as a direct result of colonization. Ross discusses how the "savage" was created in Montana through policies and racialized ideology. Native Americans in Montana have experienced warfare, genocide, and assimilation efforts. We have survived because we are a resilient people who have been able to adapt to the onslaught against us, our culture, and our very existence. Ross divides the racializing of Natives in Montana into the following: the theft of Native resources, the creation of Native deviance, the resistance by Natives to Euro-American policies and laws, and the social interaction between Natives and whites.

Native resources included land, animals, such as deer and buffalo, as well as plants, roots, and berries. Native Americans lost the means to feed their people foods that had sustained them for generations. The traditional ways of getting food for Native Americans involved travel and migration with the seasons. They began to lose traditional ways of teaching their children about the hunt and the gathering of food. Every aspect of feeding their people involved ceremony. The songs, stories, and education of generations on the importance of cultural traditions to maintain balance in the world began to be lost (Ross 1998).

Colonization greatly impacted the spiritual practices of all Native people and no less so the Natives of Montana. Once gold was discovered Congress designated it as the Montana Territory, resulting in swift population growth (Spence 1975). Native people became imprisoned in spirit and in body, with the federal government legally exercising cultural oppression enforced by local and state laws (Niezen 2000). Native people living on reservations fell under the condign power of both the Bureau of Indian Affairs and religious agents. President Ulysses S. Grant's 1868 peace policy placed religious men, nominated by churches, to oversee the Indian agencies on reservations in order to teach Christianity to Native people. Evangelism was rampant in Indian Country as it was thrown open to missionaries from a variety of mainstream churches. Catholics, Methodists, and Quakers were allowed access to Indian Country in Montana. These "Spirit Wars," as written about by Niezen (2000), show the efforts of the government and missionaries to suppress Native spiritual beliefs and practices to further the domination of Native people.

The social interaction between Natives and whites was primarily based on goals of assimilation. Ross (1998) stresses that since first contact, Natives have been treated as inferior both intellectually and culturally. Colonization resulted in extreme efforts to assimilate Native people into the dominant society. By the time the land now known as Montana was opened after gold was discovered, Native people of Montana were under siege. European invasion had brought epidemic diseases such as tuberculosis, cholera, influenza, measles, and smallpox. Montana Natives had nothing to fight these diseases as they had not yet developed the physiological immunities against them, resulting in an immeasurable number of deaths.

The Native American ways of living, being, and doing were considered inferior. They were characterized as unintelligent savages who were lazy and untrustworthy. Ross (1998) emphasizes that it was not just the theft of their resources that was used to control Native people; their behaviors were legally controlled with the use of laws and special policies and regulations. A prime example is the pass system. Native people, who for generations had lived, traveled, fed their people, and held ceremonies in sacred places, became segregated on reservations. They were required to obtain a pass to leave their reservation legally. If caught without a pass they were convicted of contravening vagrancy laws. They were criminalized for traveling in their own homelands. It was just the beginning of the criminalizing process.

MONTANA AND CRIMINALIZATION OF THE INDIAN

The first Native woman incarcerated in Montana was a Cree woman, Madeline Trottier. Ross (1998) tells us that Trottier was described as a "half-breed Indian" who was convicted of rape. Her husband was jailed for the rape of a "half-breed girl" and was allegedly accompanied by a "half-breed girl." Madeline Trottier was charged with being an accessory to the crime and sentenced to six years. Almost three years into her sentence the warden asked the governor to release Trottier and the only other female prisoner. In asking for her release, he cited the conditions of the prison and the probability that Trottier did not commit a crime. He felt she was entitled to some leniency, based on her ignorance as an Indian and that she was not expected to have knowledge about high morals. The governor denied the request for pardon in part because it would anger the white citizens of Montana.

Montana incarcerates Native Americans at a disproportionate rate compared to other races. The Prison Policy Initiative provides the following statistics: Native Americans make up 6 percent of the Montana population but are 20 percent of the total incarcerated in the state. Specifically, Native American women are 6 percent of the population of Montana but are 32 percent of the incarcerated women in the state (Wagner 2004). Native Americans in Montana are incarcerated at a rate more than four times higher than the white residents. Statistics from Montana Department of Corrections (MDOC) for the year 2014 show that 35.8 percent of the female inmate population was classified as American Indian in a total female population of 1,045 (MDOC 2015, A-17). The MDOC report acknowledges the over-representation of American Indians in the corrections system. Regarding race distribution of Montana adult offenders in 2014, MDOC provides a report on the breakdown by tribal affiliation. The Chippewa Cree, Salish-Kootenai, and Blackfeet make up more than half of the total American Indian population throughout the correction system, including male inmates (MDOC 2015, A-16). The Chippewa Cree are my people, and I will share more about our history and culture later, where I situate myself in the research.

Per the Montana Department of Corrections (2015) report, the women incarcerated in the system have a variety of programs available to them; they are housed at the Montana Women's Prison (MWP), which is said to be based on a therapeutic community model as part of the process of preparing women for reentry to their communities. The women have access to several programs, including chemical dependency, education, vocational, and parenting programs. The MWP system claims that more than 90 percent of all offenders are involved in educational, vocational, and therapeutic programs (Montana Women's Prison 2022). There is a grant-funded program conducted in collaboration with the Montana Department of Labor, the Billings Area Reentry Task Force, and Montana State University–Billings; the collaboration works with offenders considered high risk to reoffend and return to prison. The collaboration's focus is on employment; family and other relationships; and housing needs during the transition from prison to the Billings community, where they will be in pre-release (MDOC 2015, 30). Additional programs focus on personal growth through spirituality, ethics and values, caring relationships, and all aspects of physical, mental, emotional, and interpersonal health (MDOC website, "MWP"). The overall stated goal is "to provide incarcerated women an opportunity to develop the necessary skills to make positive changes in their thinking, behavior and lifestyle to successfully live as positive and productive citizens after they transition to their home communities" (MDOC 2015, 31). After serving Native American women incarcerated in Oregon, I have learned that what correction systems publicize about programs is vastly different when it comes to the actual number of women who are allowed access to programs. Definitive numbers are rarely available, and that holds true in examining the information provided by MWP and MDOC.

While not as comprehensive as their program descriptions, MWP does provide access to spiritual services for Native American women incarcerated at MWP through talking circle and sweat ceremonies. However, I was unable to obtain detailed information on how often ceremonies are held at the prison. After doing an exhaustive search I was unable to locate any transition programs in Montana dedicated to serving Native American women.

PRISON CONDITIONS IN OREGON, MONTANA, AND CANADA

I will never forget the first time I spent an entire day at the Coffee Creek Correctional Facility. I had gone in to assist with ceremony on both the minimum and medium sides of the prison. We were conducting a sweat lodge and would therefore be there for the day, including eating lunch. We went through the food line with our prison food trays and cups of water and sat down to eat with the women. On our tray was an orange which looked a bit beyond its prime, something resembling fish sticks, and a canned bean vegetable. The fish stick was beyond questionable, so I didn't touch it. I could not quite figure out the canned beans. They did not look like green beans and they did not look like yellow beans. The color and its gradation were quite strange. I ate only the orange. Later on I found out that yes, those were green beans, but they were so beyond their "consume by" date that they had lost all their color.

The Associated Press reports that during the same time period, a former Oregon prison food administrator, Farhad "Fred" Monem and his wife were indicted on bribery and money laundering charges, accused of taking more than $1 million in illegal payments and kickbacks from at least two national wholesalers of discounted foods ("Ex-buyer for Prison, Wife Accused of Taking Bribes," *Spokesman-Review*, October 20, 2007). Monem had been praised by the State of Oregon for the vast amount of money he was saving for the Oregon Department of Corrections. He boasted about using special procurement rules to pursue distressed and bulk foods aggressively on the spot market. These savings have helped Oregon regularly rank among the lowest in the nation for per-inmate food costs, and now we know why.

I often hear people say things like, "Well, they are getting three squares a day," when they are commenting on the lives of inmates. Yes, they get fed every day, but the general public is unaware of the quality of that food. In 2019 a reporter updated a 2017 story on the ongoing issue of the food being served to inmates in Oregon (Maxine Bernstein, "Four State Prisons Served Inmates Food 'Not for Human Consumption,' Lawsuit Alleges," *Oregonian*, January 9, 2019). Current and former inmates at four state prisons have filed a class action lawsuit alleging they were forced to eat fish and chicken intended as "bait food," spoiled milk, and other moldy food at four state prisons, as well as chicken and fish marked "not for human consumption." They say prior to state health inspections they were also directed to clean up kitchens and remove "not for human consumption" food, and to move green meat and other moldy, spoiled food to mobile refrigerator and freezer trucks and then to return the spoiled food to the kitchen after inspection. Make no mistake, inedible food is a human rights issue and is not the only example of harmful conditions at CCCF.

The American Civil Liberties Union (ACLU) of Montana outlines in its 2015 report *Locked in the Past* a plethora of issues throughout the Montana Department of Corrections regarding the physical conditions for prisoners. These ranged from poor quality food to inadequate basic necessities like natural light and exercise, and to sanitation problems like substandard plumbing and mold (ACLU 2015). These are just some of the examples of the human rights issues prevalent in the Montana Department of Correction facilities.

A columnist for the *Toronto Star,* Vicky Mochama, says, "To look at the experiences of women in federal prisons is to hold up a mirror and a magnifying glass to the failures of Canada's social safety net," and that "the process of incarceration treats women in an inappropriately and additionally punitive way. From a lack of mental health and drug use supports, to a dearth of meaningful opportunities for work, women's experience of the carceral system is a human rights travesty" (Mochama 2018). The Canadian Senate Committee on Human Rights affirmed Mochama's view when it studied the human rights of prisoners in the federal correctional system on a fact-finding mission between May 15 and May 19, 2017, to investigate access to mental health treatment and the effect of segregation and the overrepresentation of minorities in prisons, among other topics (Canadian Senate Committee on Human Rights 2017). They found violence, sadism, abusive guards, and volatile prisoners confined together in an oppressive and dysfunctional maze of iron and concrete.

The most heinous human rights violation that women experience in prison is that of sexual assault. There is no prison, no country, and no culture where it does not occur. While sexual assault does occur on a prisoner-to-prisoner basis, predominantly sexual assault occurs at the hands of those administrating the system. Here I highlight three stories of sexual assault, but it is critical to note that not all acts of sexual assaults by system perpetrators are reported.

Whitney Woodworth of the *Salem Statesman Journal* reported on the ongoing issue of sexual assault at the Coffee Creek Correctional Facility, citing the experience of an inmate who related that "for months a corrections officer brought drugs into the prison for her to sell, smuggled her a cell phone and had sex with her and another female inmate on two occasions" (Woodworth 2020). Woodworth reports, "Sex abuse and misconduct cases, including about 10 active lawsuits against the state, have plagued the Wilsonville prison since it opened in 2001 and through seven superintendent changes," adding, "Multiple criminal charges have been filed over the years, accusing various corrections officers and prison staff of sexually abusing inmates, coercing them to have sex in exchange for drugs and smuggling drugs inside the prison." Woodworth reminds us that this is not a new occurrence but rather part of a series of scandals involving corrections officers, staff, and outside contractors. No matter what the individual circumstances, these acts cannot be considered consensual, as the law states that an inmate cannot consent to sexual contact behind bars. In 2005 Oregon became one of the last states to enact a custodial sexual abuse law. Furthermore, beyond the legality of the acts, given the position of power prison employees hold over inmates, it is doubtful whether such acts could ever be considered consensual.

Aja Goare of MTN News covered the story of Chanda Kline, a former inmate at Montana Women's Prison who suffered sexual abuse while incarcerated (Goare 2018). She was raped by a guard and then intimidated by him for months, forcing her to keep quiet. Goare reports that Kline is certainly not the only woman who has suffered sexual abuse while being incarcerated at the Montana Women's Prison and that documents filed with Montana Public Safety Officer Standards and Training (POST) show detailed allegations against four detention officers over a period of many years.

The prison's warden, Jennie Hansen, asserts that the prison is committed to following all fifty-two standards of the Prison Rape Elimination Act. Hansen, who was hired in November 2017, says the women's prison is the only facility in the state of Montana that has passed two audits; audits are conducted every two years by an independent auditor. Goare found at the time of the report that the most recently received audit was from 2016. While the facility passed the audit, they were also in "incompliance" with several standards. A crucial standard with which they were incompliant was the protection against retaliation for inmates who report sexual abuse.

In 2019 the *Truro Daily* reported a male guard at the Nova Institution for Women in Truro being accused of "systemic sexual misconduct and abuse" against three inmates at the facility (Sullivan 2019). Accusing the state of neglect, three women filed lawsuits against the attorney general of Canada at the Nova Scotia Supreme Court in Halifax. The women allege that the guard made sexual advances, sexually abused them, and conducted sexual assaults. The guard was able to remain an employee after the women reported the abuse; according to the suit, the employee was allowed to remain employed after the allegations were made, "thereby permitting him to continue to exercise his power and control over the female inmates," and the complaint says he was eventually placed on leave but he has since retired.

A follow-up news release from the Elizabeth Fry Society said it has also been working closely with women at Nova Institution who have reported sexual assaults by a correctional officer. Emma Halpern, the executive director of the Elizabeth Fry Society of Mainland Nova Scotia, is quoted as saying, "The women launching these lawsuits suffered egregious harm at the hands of a predator who operated without reprisal, for many years, within one of our government institutions. These women reported the abuse to authorities at Nova and were ignored, transferred and made to apologize for the harms perpetrated against them. This is a clear example of the way prisons fail to keep women safe and highlights the need for women to be out of prison and receiving supportive programs in community." Halpern believes that filing of the lawsuits will be a "catalyst to create much-needed changes to Canada's policy of locking up its most vulnerable women in oppressive, toxic environments that are ripe for abuse of power" (Kirkup and MacDonald 2019).

BARBARA—KLAMATH

I first met Barbara when she was incarcerated at the Coffee Creek Correctional Facility. Barbara has graciously chosen to share some of her story. At the time we met she had served fifteen years of a seventeen-year sentence and was thirty-four years old. Barbara was first involved in the criminal justice system beginning at age thirteen. She was put in a foster home at the age of twelve because her mother was a drug addict and an alcoholic who abused her children.

Barbara was in a series of foster homes in northeast Portland, Oregon. The families with whom she was in foster care were Black families involved in the Kerby Block Crips. She was drawn to the gang experience, the concept of "where you go, I go," and a sense of belonging to something. Barbara was a runner. She ran away numerous times from her foster homes. She recalls overhearing her foster mother talking about how she got more per month for Barbara than the other foster kids who were not labeled as "rebellious," and how because of that, the foster mother would always take Barbara back, and she did.

Barbara and I discussed how flawed the foster care system was and is, in that no caseworker or judge ever asked her why she kept running. As she continued to run she would be sent back to foster care until she was sent to what was then known as Juvenile Detention Hall (JDH), which now operates as the Donald E. Long Juvenile Detention Facility. She racked up so many runaway charges that a judge sentenced her to what was then the Hillcrest School for Girls, located in Salem, Oregon. Hillcrest was a reform school for girls that eventually became coed and is now closed. Barbara was thirteen years old when she was sentenced to be incarcerated at Hillcrest until she reached her twenty-first birthday. She remembers her grandma yelling and crying when the sentence came down, and Barbara had no idea that Hillcrest was not a group home. Barbara did well there in terms of behavior until she was fifteen years old. She began to learn a lot from the older girls about life and being in the world; they pointed out that there were no fences or guards and intimated that Barbara could just leave. She asked around to other kids trying to find out if they could just leave. After a couple of weeks Barbara decided she was going to leave.

To go on a field trip you had to have a "green dot" on your identification. The green dot signified you were in good standing and could participate in off-site activities. This was Barbara's introduction to the "status" system, and she would not be free of it for more than two decades. Barbara signed up to go on a field trip to see a play in downtown Salem. On the way she told a couple of her friends about her decision to leave. They were astonished by the idea. But they decided that they too were going to leave. As soon as the van parked to let them off to go to the theater, the three of them took off walking. A staff person yelled, asking them what they were doing, and Barbara indicated that they were leaving. Barbara was quite surprised to be told that no, they could not leave, and to get back with the group. Barbara and her friends decided they had better run, which they did, while the staff person was yelling that the police were being called. Barbara yelled back, "I thought we could leave!" The three of them separated. The other two girls were caught. Barbara managed to escape. She spoke to both her aunt and her grandma on the telephone and informed them that she was not going to turn herself in. They provided her with a bus ticket, and she made her way back to Portland.

Soon Barbara was sixteen years old, pregnant, and wanted for running away. Her grandma advised her to turn herself in because the system would catch up with her when it came time for her to give birth. Barbara called her probation officer, who had not heard from Barbara since she was sentenced to Hillcrest. Barbara was informed that she would get picked up and would receive some more time. She told the probation officer that no, she was not going to have any of those things happen and, in her words, said, "Let's skip all that because I will run away again." The probation officer called her back a long three or four hours later to tell Barbara that she was free.

When the probation officer came for her home visit, she brought a new officer with her, as she was retiring. The apartment Barbara was living in was approved, and plans were made to assist Barbara in getting ready for the baby. The new probation officer followed up with Barbara and asked questions about the father of the baby, such as name, address, and age. When Barbara provided the information, the new probation officer realized that Barbara was sixteen and the father was eighteen, and all hell broke loose! Barbara was told that the father would be charged with statutory rape. Since Barbara was a ward of the state, Barbara would not have her housing or benefits approved.

She called her former probation officer, who advised that if Barbara got married upon turning seventeen years old, the system couldn't intervene.

Barbara seemingly cooperated with her probation officer until the day she turned seventeen, when she got married. Upon hearing from Barbara that she was now seventeen and married, her probation officer was livid, but it did not matter because legally Barbara was free from the system. Barbara had always been gang affiliated, as was her husband. Barbara would move to Mexico for a year with her husband and infant son, but she would come back to Portland, and they would cease contact.

Barbara was selling drugs as a way to make a living. She says they "thought they were all that with their beepers" ruling the streets. Barbara received a gun charge for being the shooter in a drive-by shooting involving another gang. She received a sentence of six months in the county jail. She now thought she was invincible, and she had been "made" as a member of the gang. She proceeded to do everything and anything that her gang was involved in, in terms of criminal activity. Barbara received thirty counts, ranging from various types of robbery to possession of a firearm, and was sentenced to seventeen years in prison; she was barely twenty years old. Later on, we will pick up on Barbara's story.

INCARCERATION OF NATIVE AMERICAN WOMEN AND JUVENILE JUSTICE

The incarceration of many Native American women began in the juvenile justice system. Wiltz (2016) states, "Native American girls are five times more likely than White girls to be incarcerated in juvenile facilities." She offers the following list, saying that Native American girls are:

More likely to be sexually abused—four times more likely than boys
More likely to end up in foster care
More likely to drop out of school
More likely to become homeless
More likely to be prey of sex traffickers
More likely than boys to end up in the adult criminal justice system
More likely to be dependent on social safety nets
More likely to have children who end up in child protective services
Five times more likely to die by age twenty-nine

More likely than white girls to be arrested for crimes that are crimes only because they are underage—called status offenses, such as running away from home or underage drinking

More likely to be arrested for family disputes

Despite some programs on tribal lands, they often find themselves without programs designed to fit their cultural background and life experiences. Wiltz shares information of a collaborative effort being conducted at the Minnesota Indian Women's Resource Center with the assistance of the Fond du Lac Band of Lake Superior Chippewa. The center seeks to leverage state, federal, and private funds to offer culturally specific programs. The programs include case management, support groups, housing, and mental health services for American Indian women and girls.

Wiltz (2016) asserts that violent crimes among Native Americans are twice as numerous as in the rest of the country. The work at the Resource Center is challenging, and Patina Park, the executive director, acknowledges how difficult it is to address the results of the poverty that has shaped their lives and made them vulnerable to prostitution, drugs, and false bonds with their abusers. However, the girls not only receive counseling, mental health services, and education counseling—they have connection to culture. Elder women teach them about "blood memory" of their ancient heritage to heal from their trauma. They learn about their cultural roots, Indian medicine, ceremony, prayer in the traditional manner, and honoring their ancestors.

Hartney (2008) provides the following factors that influence Native American system involvement:

Poverty: Native Americans are among the most impoverished racial groups in the U.S. and have the second highest percentage of families living below the federal poverty level. (U.S. Census Bureau 2004, cited in Hartney 2008, 5).

Education: In the last U.S. Census, Native Americans reported a lower level of education attainment in comparison to the general U.S. population, with 29.1 percent of Native Americans not graduating from high school (U.S. Census Bureau 2006, cited in Hartney 2008, 5).

Furthermore, "Native American youth were victimized at greater rates than other youth. The 2002 annual average violent victimization against youth (aged 12–17 years)" disproportionately affects Native American youth, who experience the highest per capita rate of violence of any racial group (Perry 2004, cited in Hartney 2008, 5).

Working with women experiencing incarceration with a goal of healing and battling recidivism requires addressing what has happened in their lives from childhood on to adulthood. Buttenwieser (2016) states, "Women behind bars are more likely than men to have a family history of substance abuse and felony convictions, to have an unstable childhood home life, and to originate from a low-income family." She goes on to say, "Women often begin their entry into the criminal justice system when they are girls. In fact, the number of girls in the juvenile justice system has been increasing steadily over the past two decades. Girls of color are also overrepresented in the juvenile justice system. For example, African American girls constitute 14 percent of girls in the U.S. but make up one third of detained and committed girls. Native American girls are 1 percent of the general population of girls but 3.5 percent of detained and committed girls."

Working with the women in the Healing the Sacred Hoop workshop, we delved into their childhood experiences in order for them to voice their experiences, come to terms with their past, and move toward healing. As Buttenwieser discussed, I found that the bulk of the women were involved in criminal activity while young, and many were in the juvenile justice system. The majority of the women had been in the foster care system.

In her article "Pathways to Prison," Dana DeHart (2008), the assistant dean for research at the University of South Carolina College of Social Work, states, "One of the most harmful aspects of our system is that we tend to criminalize women's survival strategies—the ways they cope with abuse and trauma. Girls may run away from home or use drugs as a means of escaping abuse—escaping physically or mentally. Then these same behaviors are considered delinquent or criminal acts." Working with incarcerated women, I have found that reasons why women and girls might become involved with illegal activity are usually still not addressed when they come into contact with the criminal justice system.

Prosecution and incarceration add to the trauma while not addressing the reasons why women and young adults come to be incarcerated.

CANADA'S CHILD-WELFARE-TO-PRISON PIPELINE

Renu Mandhane, the chief commissioner of the Ontario Human Rights Commission, spoke on the *Nation to Nation* news show about the issue of First Nations children who have been involved in Ontario's child welfare population having a large presence in the juvenile justice system (Mandhane 2020). She terms this connection "child-welfare-to-prison pipeline" and cites the experiences of institutionalization as beginning in the child welfare system. The child welfare system did not give these children the opportunity or capacity to obtain an education or live an independent life. As in the United States, many of these children who begin in the juvenile justice system then move on to the adult systems of incarceration.

THE U.S. SCHOOL-TO-PRISON PIPELINE

In "Trauma-Informed Education: Addressing School-to-Prison Pipeline," Ashley Benton (2019) addresses childhood trauma and its causal impact on the school-to-prison pipeline. She cites research by the Third National Incidence Study of Child Abuse and Neglect, which reveals that that almost three times as many children are maltreated as are reported to Child Protective Services. The research finds that multiple adverse childhood experiences (ACEs) cause people to develop attitudes and beliefs about both their experiences and themselves that can lead to life-long depression and self-harming behaviors. These experiences result in children feeling anxious, guarded, and easily triggered. ACEs inhibit children's ability to learn, their ways to deal with conflict, and their capacity to develop healthy relationships. They can erroneously blame themselves for their adverse experiences, and they often internalize the abuse that they have suffered.

Benton shares a speech given by California's surgeon general, Dr. Nadine Harris, who said, "We now understand better than we ever have before how exposure to early adversity affects the developing brains and bodies of children. It affects the pleasure and reward center of the brain that is implicated in substance dependence. It inhibits the prefrontal cortex, which is necessary for impulse control and executive function, a critical area for learning. And on MRI scans we see measurable differences in the amygdala, the brain's fear response center" (Benton 2019). The time between early childhood and adolescence is a critical developmental period, for more than academic learning. It is a crucial time for socioemotional development. The negative impacts of trauma include impacts on the ability to learn and perform in school. These children often fall through the cracks of traditional public educational systems.

One of the most significant differences in approach between traditional ways of learning for Indigenous children and traditional public educational systems is the punitive approach. Benson describes these systems as having "punitive disciplinary responses rather than restorative, further damaging and effectively pushing traumatized children away from education systems rather than bringing them in." Benton asserts that if those students involved in truancy and exhibiting behavioral issues are instead screened for ACEs, and if educators are trained in trauma-informed approaches, it would ensure that all students are learning and would create a shift from the school-to-prison pipeline toward more successful school and life experiences. Benton shares the definition of the school-to-prison pipeline and the theory of cause by the American Bar Association (ABA): "For far too many students, entering the gateway to incarceration begins with a referral from the classroom to the courtroom. This phenomenon is referred to as the school-to-prison pipeline." The NAACP Legal Defense Fund described this pipeline as "funneling of students out of school and into the streets and the juvenile correction system." There are two main contributing factors that have led to the expansion of the school-to-prison pipeline: (1) school disciplinary practices, and (2) zero tolerance policies (Tyner 2021).

This leads to harsh policies, often misapplied, increasing the probabilities that students will end up in the juvenile correction system. Benton provides the following statistics supporting this perspective from the ABA: "Nationally, a public student is suspended every second and a half. This equates to 3.3 million children being suspended each year. One study found that 95 percent of out-of-school suspensions were for nonviolent, minor disruptions such as tardiness or disrespect. Previous studies have shown that even a single suspension can double the odds of that student later dropping out—missed days in the classroom plus missed learning opportunity equals a decreased likelihood of a student's ability to complete high school successfully and enter the pipeline to higher education."

Benton refers to research done by NPR ED showing solid evidence in support of the positive impact of trauma-informed education and restorative practices to children (Kamenetz 2017). She holds the belief that although these are relatively new concepts, there is both research and momentum to adopt these practices. Benton says:

> The hope is to reach all children, especially those who in older models have been left behind. By teaching concepts relative to mindfulness, neuroplasticity, and identifying parts of the brain responsible for decision making, memory, and emotion (how they are working together), educators have an opportunity to develop rapport with their students, while teaching skills for resiliency and emotional regulation. Children who are able to identify how they feel and why they experience certain emotions can then develop skills to become better communicators. They can decide on healthy narratives which allows them to feel more autonomous and ultimately make better decisions. Applying these skills can begin to help students experiencing trauma by allowing them to feel less on edge in the classroom and primed for learning. . . . In considering these new approaches, we can ensure we educate traumatized children, address mental health, and reduce the number of students pushed out of the education system and into incarceration. (Benton 2019)

The negative practices discussed by Benton as traditional educational practices in this country are diametrically opposed to traditional ways of learning for Native people. I remember my grandfather George Denny telling me about traditional ways of learning for Cree children. First of all, we learned many things at the knees of our grandmothers, grandfathers, and Elders. Children were shown how to do things. If a mistake was made, rather than saying a child had done something wrong, the mentor gently took the child's hands and showed how to do the task.

This was done as often as needed, and there were no recriminations. If the learning was verbal, it would be repeated, and it was a process that included respect for the child and honored the relationship between the student and teacher.

Native girls and women often come from homes of poverty where family violence is prevalent. Children living in violent homes find a multitude of ways to cope. Unfortunately, many of these ways of coping are not positive, as described by the Domestic Abuse Intervention Project. They suggest that living with a parent using violence has the following effects: violence at school, truancy, running away, teen pregnancy, use of pornography, date rape, sexual harassment, sexual assault, food addictions, substance abuse, violence on the streets, and new generations of violent families (National Center on Domestic and Sexual Violence 2017).

Native American children have a high rate of violent homes, and the women in the Healing the Sacred Hoop workshop used many of the coping mechanisms described by the Domestic Abuse Intervention Project. Unfortunately, those who were mothers themselves were often unable to provide healthy nonviolent homes for their children. The cycle of abuse, violence, and incarceration will continue unless culturally specific programming is available to juvenile and adult offenders.

THE PRISON EXPERIENCE

It is important for those of us on the outside to consider what prison is like to an inmate. Coffee Creek Correctional Facility (CCCF) provides the following information on the State of Oregon website: "CCCF is a multi-custody prison accommodating all of the State of Oregon female inmates. It provides intake and evaluation of all female and male inmates committed to state custody by the courts. The prison has cell and dormitory housing, inmate work programs, skills training, education, treatment programs, health services, religious services, physical plant, warehouse space for on-site storage, a central records unit, and administration areas" (ODOC 2022). While it is evident that the women at CCCF have numerous opportunities for activities, there are no statistics available on which groups and activities the women are attending. In addition, one's sentence, classification as an inmate, and designation in terms of conduct and compliance determine one's opportunity to take part in activities. In terms of vocational programs, a very small percentage of women can take part in those programs. Participation is based on conduct and compliance as well as capacity within each program.

In contrast, the Montana Women's Prison website provides the following information: "Montana Women's Prison in Billings is a 194-bed secure facility that operates consistently at or over capacity, with approximately 200 female felony inmates. The state-run facility provides a secure environment that emphasizes accountability, productivity and personal growth. Montana Women's Prison has a staff of about 92, including 20 contract personnel" (MWP 2022). We cannot personally know what the day in the life of an inmate looks like, what governs how inmates spend their time, or what it feels like to have one's day dictated by an institution for twenty-four hours a day, seven days a week. We can only try to imagine that experience. And we should bear in mind that while there are set times for certain things such as the "count," happenings inside a prison may change drastically depending on two major factors: (a) whether a prison is in "lockdown" due to a fight, perceived threat, or system disruption, and (b) the fact that activities can be cancelled by the prison for any reason they deem necessary.

RECOVERY-REENTRY, MONTANA

According to the Montana Women's Prison website, they provide an environment that is designed to improve outcomes for women's recovery and reentry into Montana communities by emphasizing personal accountability, public safety, and restorative justice for crime victims (MWP 2022).

The federal Substance Abuse and Mental Health Services Administration (SAMSA) defines "recovery" as a process of change through which individuals improve their health and wellness, live a self-directed life, and strive to reach their full potential. The state-run prison's operation utilizes a recovery-reentry model as part of the process for preparing women for reentry into their communities. Programs that are available to the women are medical and dental services, mental health treatment, chemical dependency counseling, educational and vocational programming, and parenting workshops. Allegedly, more than 90 percent of all inmates at the Women's Prison are involved in educational, vocational, and recovery-reentry programming; however, it is questionable that 180 out of 200 inmates (at the time of writing) are in line in terms of conduct and compliance and therefore able to access this programming.

The prison strives to promote child-parent bonding and development of parenting skills in preparation for family reunification. Special family "Kids' Day" events occur once a month under the supervision of parenting staff to promote positive relationships. The prison's educational programs include classes to obtain high school–equivalency diplomas, college preparation classes, and courses to learn computer, personal, and job-related skills. In partnership with the prison, correctional enterprises offer inmates vocational training opportunities through the prison industries program. Industries include garment and apparel screen printing, direct printing, design work, and embroidery as well as assembling hygiene kits for prisoners. The prison paws program was started in 2004. It is a canine training program that allows inmates an opportunity to learn new skills and improve self-esteem while socializing dogs and teaching them basic manners, so that the canines are better community members. A garden project, launched in 2012, has enhanced the nutritional variety available to inmates, and when an abundance of produce is available donations are made to the community food bank. The women who work in the garden and greenhouse can earn their master gardener certification in addition to life-skills and technical on-the-job training in greenhouse operations.

The programs offered by the prison are enhanced by community partnerships and the large number of volunteers who donate time to bring in activities and workshops on topics including spirituality, physical well-being, substance abuse treatment, healthy relationships, cognitive behavioral strategies, creative arts, and victim awareness. Victims who participate in restorative justice programs such as a victim awareness panel often experience healing; and it strengthens inmates' accountability and understanding of the harm they created through their crime while promoting a social bond to the community. These programs encourage change in inmates and provide ties to community, while allowing them to give back in a positive and productive way through interactions and community service projects.

The Billings Area Reentry Task Force is a collaborative partnership made up of community stakeholders. The task force consists of the Montana Department of Labor, Montana State University–Billings, Montana Department of Corrections, other government entities, faith- and community-based organizations, and other interested local parties who promote the removal of barriers that may impede successful offender reentry. This holistic approach starts at the point of contact with the criminal justice system, focusing on employment, family and other relationships, health services, alcohol and other drug treatment, and housing needs during an inmate's transition from prison to the community (MWP 2022).

The Montana State Department of Corrections, unlike Oregon, does have an American Indian liaison, Harlan Trombley (Blackfeet), who began with the Department of Corrections in 2013 in what was a new role. *Correctional News* cited his job as "a link between law enforcement and American Indian offenders, their families, the Office of Indian Affairs, tribal councils and others" (December 4, 2013, cited in MDOC 2015)— the technical advisor to department staff regarding issues related to American Indian offenders.

According to the Montana Department of Corrections *2015 Biennial Report*, since he joined the department in November 2013, the liaison has

> traveled extensively, setting up regular monthly meetings with staff and American Indian offenders in state and contract facilities, treatment programs and prerelease centers throughout the state. In addition to meeting with adult offenders, the liaison regularly meets with American Indian youths in the state's two juvenile correctional facilities. The liaison also has traveled to each of the reservations with the Governor's Director of Indian Affairs and the program manager for the State Tribal Economic Development Commission. At meetings with tribal council members, the liaison discussed his role within the corrections system and encouraged the tribes to support a mentoring program at the Montana State Prison and to involve more volunteers from tribal reservations in assisting and supporting offenders throughout the system. (MDOC 2015, 8)

While it is good to learn that there is a formal liaison, I was unfortunately unable to speak with him, although I left numerous messages. I would have liked to ask him, among other things:

What has been the response from the tribes in terms of offering a mentoring program to Native Americans incarcerated in the state of Montana?

In Oregon there are many Native American Elders who would like to be part of the volunteer spiritual program but cannot because they are unable to pass the background check. Does he experience the same difficulty in Montana?

Although the work of the Native American spiritual volunteers is respected at many of the correctional facilities in Oregon, there are still difficulties in adherence to protocol when it comes to the handling of sacred objects during the processing of volunteers and guests. Does he hear of the same difficulty in his role as the tribal liaison, and has the staff training he has been doing made a difference in how corrections staff interact with inmates and volunteers?

I am hopeful that sometime in the future I can have a conversation with him while doing future research.

The Oregon Department of Corrections does not have a designated tribal liaison, something that was advocated for by the Native American Advisory Council, of which I was a member. We were a self-formed group who made it impossible for the ODOC to ignore us. We demanded time with the ODOC, and frankly, they were afraid of a lawsuit, as our initial concerns were about religious rights. We formed in response to the mishandling of sacred items, the enforcement of the Native American Religious Freedom Act, and poor behavior by institutional employees in relation to Native American culture.

RECOVERY-REENTRY, CANADA

The Correctional Service of Canada provides the following information about their Indigenous reintegration program:

The Correctional Service of Canada (CSC) works with Indigenous communities throughout Canada to enhance the role of Indigenous communities in corrections and reintegrate Indigenous offenders into Indigenous communities.

The Aboriginal Community Reintegration Program allows communities to take part in the release and reintegration planning process. Offenders can ask for support from an Indigenous community at any point during their sentence.

Section 84 of the Corrections and Conditional Release Act legislates the process for releasing an offender into an Indigenous community. The offender must give consent. At that point CSC can give advance notice of their parole application to the community.

HOW THE PROCESS WORKS

The steps in the program are:

1. CSC informs Indigenous federal offenders of Section 84 and the process involved. If the offenders would like to take part then they must write to the community they have chosen to ask for support.
2. CSC contacts the community to discuss the process.
3. If the community agrees, they work with CSC to plan for the offender's release. Note: The community may request funding support by submitting a proposal. The proposal should be a 2 to 3 page submission outlining the proposed involvement of the community, describing the nature of community support, and outlining the funding requirements to support preparation of a release plan.

Path Home: Release Planning Kit—Section 84 of the Corrections and Conditional Release Act further explains how CSC works with Indigenous communities throughout Canada.

FINANCIAL AID

CSC wants to ensure that costs are not an impediment to Indigenous communities' participation in the conditional release of Indigenous offenders.

Sometimes Indigenous communities or organizations lack the resources to address offender needs. In these cases, CSC can work with the community to link them with the necessary resources. The parole officer or the Indigenous community development officer can provide a referral if needed.

Examples of expenses that available funding may cover include transportation expenses for community resource people travelling to institutions to work with offenders and parole officers (e.g., community staff, Chief, councillors, Elders) or preparations in the community for the eventual release date (e.g., reintegration circles). (https://www.csc-scc.gc.ca)

Looking at the information from the website of Correctional Service Canada, it is clear that there has been much more effort made to work with the First Nations people of Canada in designing a reentry program. One of the remarkable differences between the Canadian system and that of Montana and Oregon is the work with the First Nations communities and the edict to offer First Nations offenders culturally responsive interventions, programs, and services. Crucial elements of their model are outlined as follows:

ELDERS

Elders and spiritual advisors guide Indigenous offenders to traditional Indigenous ways of life, based on their own teachings. They work both individually and in groups using teachings, counselling, and traditional ceremonies and practices.

The defining characteristics of an Elder are their knowledge and wisdom of traditional ways, and the respect of the people within the community, identified by community members.

Elders follow a traditional way of life and have been following the teaching of Elders and healers over a significant period of time. Some Elders may have additional attributes, such as those of a traditional healer.

Services that an Elder or spiritual advisor may offer to offenders include group sessions (circles) and individual discussions with offenders in the institution; spiritual services and various traditional ceremonies; helping offenders follow a healing path that supports their correctional plan; escorting offenders on escorted temporary absences (ETA) for ceremonial and other spiritual purposes; and advising institutions on ceremonies and ceremonial objects, traditional practices and protocols, traditional medicines, or sacred ground within the institution.

Forum on Corrections Research explains the tradition and holistic approach of Elders. It discusses the validity of diagnoses, cultural competence, and programs for Indigenous offenders.

Elder Vulnerability within CSC summarizes recommendations and action plans that are areas of concerns and vulnerabilities of Elders working with CSC.

INDIGENOUS STAFF

Learn about the staff who specialize in helping Indigenous offenders find a more traditional path to healing.

INDIGENOUS LIAISON OFFICERS

Indigenous liaison officers (ILOs) work closely with Elders / spiritual advisors. They ensure that the case management team understands the offender's work with the Elder / spiritual advisor and help the Elder / spiritual advisor and support work with Indigenous offenders wherever possible.

INDIGENOUS CORRECTIONAL PROGRAM OFFICERS

Indigenous correctional program officers (ICPOs) are part of the case management team. They contribute to the healing journey of Indigenous offenders, address, in a culturally sensitive manner, an offender's behaviors that may potentially lead to reoffending, and provide the required programming to address the needs identified in healing plans.

INDIGENOUS COMMUNITY DEVELOPMENT OFFICERS

Indigenous community development officers (ICDOs) work with Indigenous offenders interested in returning to their communities. Through the Section 84 process, ICDOs also assist in building positive partnerships between Indigenous communities and CSC.

INDIGENOUS COMMUNITY LIAISON OFFICERS

Indigenous community liaison officers (ICLOs) work from the community. They monitor, support, and motivate Indigenous offenders in individual and/or group settings, and work with Elders to facilitate, organize, and coordinate Indigenous culture, traditional/spiritual ceremonies, social activities, and programs.

REGIONAL PATHWAYS COORDINATORS

Regional Pathways coordinators help to develop and monitor the Pathways Initiative and its results. They ensure the cultural appropriateness and competence of Pathways operations, interventions, and services.

INSTITUTIONAL PATHWAYS COORDINATORS

An institutional Pathways coordinator (IPC) works at any institution with forty or more Pathways participants. The IPC coordinates Indigenous services, activities, and interventions in collaboration with the Elder, institutional management, and the regional Pathways coordinator.

NATIONAL ABORIGINAL ADVISORY COMMITTEE

The National Aboriginal Advisory Committee (NAAC) provides advice to CSC on correctional policies and practices related to reintegration of Indigenous offenders. It provides expertise on Indigenous issues like northern community strategies, cultural awareness training, nationhood, electronic monitoring, offender aftercare for Indigenous offenders, and employment needs in the community.

One of the goals of my work is to "make the invisible visible," and to that end it is imperative that those with no knowledge or experience of the issue of incarceration of Native American women are given a lens through which to see the women and avail themselves of some of the historical background of Native American people. The general public often only has the "mythical" version of the history of our people, as taught in public school and viewed from Hollywood movies. Additionally, until anyone, Native or not, has been inside a prison, worked or volunteered within the prison system, or had a family member or close friend in prison, it is impossible truly to understand the system, much less its effects on those who are incarcerated. As a society, we are bombarded at the beginning of any news broadcast with stories of crimes of the day. Those stories help shape how we view those who are deemed criminals. Elected representatives and those running for office are called upon to be "tough on crime," and to be considered "soft on crime" is viewed as not wanting to protect the public. Looking at the websites of corrections departments summarized here, it may seem as though people who are imprisoned are actively engaged in educational, vocational, spiritual, and rehabilitative activities all day long; in reality, not only does the system regulate their day but opportunities for self-work are determined by their status as inmates and are often determined by contemptuous corrections employees. The prison system itself is complex, as is its history.

CHAPTER 2

Law and Policy in Native American History

Vine Deloria Jr. (Standing Rock Sioux) was a Native American theologian, historian, professor, activist, and prolific writer. Deloria's first book, *Custer Died for Your Sins* (1969), forced the reading public to recognize stereotypes of Native Americans, while challenging white audiences to take a new look at the history of the western expansion of the United States and to become aware of the abuses of Native Americans. Deloria asserted that the disastrous policy of termination was conceived with the thought that it would provide the elusive "answer" to the Indian problem. On June 9, 1953, the House Concurrent Resolution 108 (HCR 108) was introduced in the Eighty-Third Congress. HCR 108 declared the intention of Congress to terminate federal supervision at the "earliest possible time" (Deloria 1969, 62).

According to the relief organization Partnership with Native Americans, "from 1953–1964, 109 tribes were terminated, and federal responsibility and jurisdiction was turned over to state governments. Approximately 2,500,000 acres of trust land were removed from protected status and 12,000 Native Americans lost tribal affiliation. The lands were sold to non-Indians and the tribes lost official recognition by the U.S. government" (Partnership with Native Americans 2022). Termination had a massive negative impact on tribes deemed eligible, primarily in education, health, and tribal economy. Prior to termination, Indian Health Services (IHS) provided health care to many tribes. Under the termination policy, most tribes were rendered ineligible and were left with no access to hospitals, clinics, or health care in general. The health of Native Americans deteriorated further, far below that of white Americans (American Indian Movement 2022).

The termination policy's negative impact was not limited to education, health, and the economy of tribes. Termination was another policy effort to force assimilation of Native people into the larger dominant culture, and on that note, it was partly successful. The greatest impact was the loss of tribal identity and cultural practices. Deloria cites the weakness of the value system of the dominant society: "When a policy is used as a weapon to force cultural confrontation, then the underlying weakness of society is apparent. No society which has real and lasting values need rely on force for their propagation" (Deloria 1969, 77).

There was more than one relocation act passed. The Indian Relocation Act of 1954 set termination policy, and the Relocation Act of 1956 provided the funding. The intention of the legislation was to convince Native Americans to leave reservations and assimilate into the urban population. The U.S. government was decreasing financial support to Native Americans living on reservations, and the Indian Relocation Act offered to pay vocational training and moving expenses to move from reservations to government-designated cities, including Denver, Chicago, Los Angeles, San Francisco, and Dallas. People were promised help in orientating to urban living as well as in financial management and vocational training and programs (Stanford Medicine 2019).

The Indian Relocation Act cannot be deemed a successful effort. Housing, vocational training, and assimilation into an urban lifestyle proved to be difficult; as the promised jobs were not there, the minimal payments toward housing did not cover expenses, and the money dried up. While it can be said that large numbers of Native Americans remained in the cities, the bulk of those ended up living in poverty with escalating alcohol and drug addictions (Ono 2004). Once again, a governmental policy further separated Native people from their families, tribes, culture, spirituality, and their land.

We need to look at history beyond the lens of the Western world. Deloria, in his book *God Is Red* (1994), explicates the difference between the Indian view of time and history and that in Western thought. The key to the difference is time: Western history is divided up by time, while Indian history is not bound by chronology. History was conveyed by important happenings from the seasonal to the experiences of our ancestors, both past and current tribal members. Examples can be found in petroglyphs, buffalo hides, and calendar sticks, to name just a few. Of equal importance are the stories passed down verbally. These stories recount hard winters, plentiful hunts, skirmishes, visions, healings, and all other aspects of tribal existence. In my family and in my tribe we learn about our ancestors from my great-great-great-grandfather Chief Black Powder, to my great-great-grandfather Chief Big Bear, to my great-grandfather Chief Little Bear. Today it is possible to find written word about all of these ancestors, but traditionally we learned about them through a verbal recounting of their lives.

Hugh Dempsey, in his book *Big Bear: The End of Freedom* (1984), relates a celebrated account of an important happening in the life of my great-great-grandfather Chief Big Bear. Big Bear was an important chief, and his supernatural powers were well known. He had received his name after he had an intense vision of the Bear Spirit, which the Cree saw as the most powerful animal spirit. Big Bear traveled to the Red Deer River to fast and to pray. While there, he had one of the most important visions of his life. The Bear Spirit told Big Bear how to make a power bundle, which he did upon his return to his village, with the assistance of medicine men, following the directions he received from the Bear Spirit. This sacred bundle would protect him and his people, and at times in his life he would be invisible in times of danger. It was made of a skinned-out bear's paw and was sewn onto red flannel. Big Bear had his power bundle with him his entire life. Today Big Bear's power bundle is in the American Museum of Natural History in New York City.

One of my relatives, Duane Grant, has seen our ancestor's power bundle and keeps abreast of efforts to bring it back to our people. He tells us that in

1988–89, a group of young Cree, including Jim Thunder and Lewis Cardinal, ran a Big Bear centenary pilgrimage on foot, 4,300 kilometers from Edmonton to New York, to try to repatriate it. However, there was strong disagreement among Big Bear's descendants, both in Canada and Montana, as to where Chief's Son's Hand should go, and so museum officials refused to release it. In September 1994, curator Stanley Fried told me: "The American Museum will do the right thing [by the bundle], once we know what the right thing is. As long as the Cree cannot agree, it will stay here." Today the bundle is no longer protected in PeeMee's original canvas bag; in fact, it is no longer a bundle. And it is no longer in a small room surrounded by hundreds of other communal Cree artifacts, the way I first saw it in June 1972. In November 2007, I found that all the museum's artifacts have been archived according to the materials of which they were made. Each of Chief's Son's Hand's nine wrapping cloths has been unleafed, numbered, and laid out separately. And I saw the ancient clawed paw as it had always been, sewn unevenly with leather thongs onto its red stroud by the Cree boy. But it now lies, numbered and naked, in a separate antiseptic drawer in the processed air of the huge museum vaults, with nothing but a twist of tobacco and a short braid of sweet grass for companionship. (Grant 2019)

It is a great sorrow that Big Bear's power bundle is not being taken care of in "a good way," and I hope we will be able to agree on who should have the bundle and have it returned in a ceremonial manner and brought back to its original form. I share this story because it is true. We as his descendants believe in the power granted to Big Bear, and we would believe it even if the power bundle was lost to us. It is more than history; it is the story and spiritual belief of our family and our people.

Another key distinction between Western history and tribal history is the dependence of religion in Western history. Western history co-mingles religion in the recounting of happenings and considers the Bible and the Torah as accurate recountings of history. Tribal history needs no outside source to anchor and validate it. Deloria states, "In a real sense, the Christian religion can be said to be dependent on the historical accuracy of the Hebrew religion as found in the sacred books of the Jews" (Deloria 1994, 104). The events in the Old Testament and the death of Jesus became "the first Christian effort to define the meaning of past events in terms of humankind's universal history" (105).

Tribal history includes the spiritual, and beliefs and spiritual happenings are important to us. There is however an important distinction when it comes to spiritual happenings and tribal history in the United States. Deloria explains, "The tribal religions had one great benefit other religions did not and could not have. They had no religious controversy within their communities because everyone shared a common historical experience and cultural identity wasn't separated into religious, economic, sociological, political, and military spheres" (Deloria 1994, 100). He continues that no tribe declared that their beliefs were right and that the beliefs of another tribe were wrong. There was not the Western way of searching for what can never be found, the absolute truth.

Roxanne Dunbar-Ortiz (2014) provides one of the most extensive, truth-telling, documented treatises on the history of the United States from an Indigenous perspective, the consequences of historical happenings, and the intent of the so-called Founding Fathers and the federal government. It would be impossible for me to convey all that the process of colonization has done to wreak havoc on the Native people of what is now the United States, much less North America and the world. However, two of the elements I want to discuss here are land and identity. Dunbar-Ortiz writes, "Under the crust of that portion of Earth called the United States of America—'from California . . . to the Gulf Stream waters'—are interred the bones, villages, fields, and sacred objects of American Indians. . . . To learn and know this history is both a necessity and a responsibility to the ancestors and descendants of all the parties" (Dunbar-Ortiz 2014, 1). She quotes historian David Chang, who tells us that "nation, race, and class converged in the land," and she reminds us that in U.S. history, "everything is about the land—who oversaw it, who cultivated it, fished its waters, maintained its wildlife; who invaded and stole it; how it became a commodity ('real estate') broken into pieces to be bought and sold on the market" (Dunbar-Ortiz 2014, 1).

CHAPTER 3

Incarceration from a Philosophical and Historical Perspective

THE PRISON SYSTEM AND FOUCAULT

Having had a glimpse of the experience of incarceration of women and the governmental policies and beliefs imposed on the Native American people, it is crucial to consider the prison system itself. Reading Luana Ross's *Inventing the Savage* (1998) caused me to do more research about the system, which led me to Michel Foucault and other authors. There has been a great deal written about the prison industrial complex; for my research, I concentrated on the experiences of women.

Reading *Discipline and Punish: The Birth of the Prison* by Foucault (1977) not only provided a historical view of punishment and incarceration; it provides a greater understanding of the sociological underpinnings. Foucault begins in the 1700s, when public punishment and execution were commonplace, as he describes the action of a body being drawn and quartered. Flesh was torn from the body, ending in the body being set on fire until only the ashes remained. He then moves the reader forward eighty years, delineating the House of Rules for young prisoners in Paris, which designated the daily timetable and activities of prisoners. Foucault states, "It was a time when, in Europe and in the United States, the entire economy of punishment was redistributed. It was a time of great 'scandals' for traditional justice, a time of innumerable projects for reform. It saw a new theory of law and crime, a new moral or political justification of the right to punish; old laws were abolished, old customs died out. 'Modern' codes were planned or drawn up. It was a new age for penal justice" (1977, 7). He cites the disappearance of torture as a public spectacle as an example of the slackening of the hold on the body. As history moved forward, the body was not touched as much as in the past, as a vehicle for torture; instead, the body began to be used as an instrument of constraints, imprisonment, to make it work, to deprive a person of liberty. He states, "The body, according to this penalty, is caught up in a system of constraints and privations, obligations, and prohibitions" (Foucault 1977, 11). The body becomes the focus of suspended rights.

The result of this change, asserts Foucault, is the creation of a legion of technicians who replace the executioner. These include wardens, doctors, chaplains, psychiatrists, psychologists, and educators, all of whom are to proclaim that the body and the application of pain to the body are no longer the objects of ultimate punitive punishment. This is not to say that execution does not still take place, but allegedly it is pain free with the injection of tranquilizers administered under the eyes of a physician. He goes on to contend that the hold on the body changed from torture and the infliction of pain to the loss of assets and rights.

Punishment in the form of forced labor and loss of liberty combined with the ration of food, deprivation of sex, corporal punishment, and solitary confinement certainly can bring physical pain along with emotional and psychological pain. Foucault says that since the focus is no longer the body or blood, it instead is replaced: "The expiation that once rained down upon the body must be replaced by a punishment that acts in depth on the heart, the thoughts, the will, the inclinations" (Foucault 1977, 16). The system of punitive justice changed, and those changes are certainly reflected in the United States criminal justice system.

In *Discipline and Punish*, Foucault asserts that judges in Europe, while setting up a new penal system in the 1700s, began judging more than the crimes of any individual; they began judging the *soul* of a criminal. Punishment becomes partly about rehabilitation. He describes a whole new process that assesses, diagnoses, prognosticates, and makes normative judgments, changing the framework of penal judgment. Foucault depicts the process as one in which looking at the crime and the criminal has added the element of looking at the perpetrator in terms of how to determine the causal processes that produced the crime. In terms of the perpetrator, this becomes an effort to look at the environment, family heredity, instinct, and soundness of mind for the punishment to include possible rehabilitation. Foucault asserts that the machinery of the criminal justice system was being developed for years around the concept of the implementation of sentences and the adjustment of sentencing due to individual conditions. The perpetrator is examined in terms of the risk to society, the susceptibility to penal punishment, curability, and the ability to readjust. The sentencing objective then becomes "the administration of the penalty, its necessity, its usefulness, its possible effectiveness, whether the mental hospital would be a more suitable place of confinement than the prison, whether this confinement should be short or long, whether medical treatment or security measures are called for" (Foucault 1977, 22). The *new* penal system created a process that allowed judges to judge more than the crime, and the change in the system created extrajudicial elements and personnel. Foucault urges us to look beyond punitive mechanisms and their repressive and punishing aspects alone, and instead to consider punishment as a complex social function. He describes a system in which "the prison form antedates its systematic use in the penal system" (231). He says that the prison was not the expression of the new policies and procedures, but rather,

> it had already been constituted outside the legal apparatus when, throughout the social body, procedures were being elaborated for distributing individuals, fixing them in space, classifying them, extracting from them the maximum in time and forces, training their bodies, coding their continuous behaviors, maintaining them in perfect visibility, forming around them an apparatus of observation, registration and recording, constituting them on them a body of knowledge that is accumulated and centralized. The general form of an apparatus intended to render individuals docile and useful, by means of precise work on their bodies. The prison, an essential element in the punitive panoply, certainly marks an important moment in the history of penal justice: its access to "humanity." But it is also an important moment in the history of those disciplinary mechanisms that

the new class of power was developing: that in which they colonized the legal system. (Foucault 1977, 231)

As a society, as a takeaway from Foucault (1977), we need to consider and examine our very thoughts and opinions about those who have committed crimes and how the systems of the judiciary and corrections should view and penalize these individuals. Are we in favor of punishment that focuses on the very heart and soul of an individual? Is anyone within the criminal justice system truly capable of judging, assessing, and diagnosing every offender to determine their risk to society and ability to be rehabilitated? Something I always ask my audiences when I speak on the issue of incarceration is, "What does a felon look like to you?" Their responses always follow along the same continuum, often describing felons as dangerous looking; they display *shady* behavior, and the way they are dressed is suspect. Frankly, race comes into it, but people tiptoe around that, unwilling to voice what they truly feel; Brown and Black people seem more dangerous. When inquiring about their feelings regarding punishment and prison, their responses show the majority as seeing the need for incarceration to protect society; the concept of "do the crime—pay the time" is a standard belief. Audiences occasionally differentiate between those convicted of murder and lesser crimes. Audience members tend to know little about the history of incarceration in this country since first contact. Additionally, their answers rarely speak of offenders as human beings. Clearly, we need to examine the very humanity of the system and our own humanity, which Foucault challenges us to do.

Foucault informs us, "The prison should not be seen as an inert institution, shaken at intervals by reform movements. The 'theory of the prison' was its constant set of operational instructions rather than its incidental criticism—one of its conditions of functioning. The prison has always formed part of an active field in which projects, improvements, experiments, theoretical statements, personal evidence and investigations have proliferated" (Foucault 1977, 235). As already noted in chapter 1, we can recognize the institutional regulation of the day-to-day life of an inmate, which Foucault describes as the function of prison:

In several respects, the prison must be an exhaustive disciplinary apparatus: it must assume responsibility for all aspects of the individual, his physical training, his aptitude to work, his everyday conduct, his moral attitude, his state of mind; the prison, much more than the school, the workshop or the army, which always involved a certain specialization is "omni-disciplinary." Moreover, the prison has neither exterior nor gap; it cannot be interrupted, except when its task is totally completed; its action on the individual must be uninterrupted; an unceasing discipline. Lastly, it gives almost total power over the prisoners; it has its internal mechanisms of repression and punishment, a despotic discipline. (Foucault 1977, 236)

It is imperative that we comprehend the concept of total power and control when we think about incarceration. It is not just the body that is locked up; in many ways it is also the mind and the soul. Society wants the offender to emerge from prison as a moral and upstanding member of society, but the prison industrial complex cannot possibly address all the contributing experiences that brought an individual to criminal behavior. The larger dominant Western culture in this country prides itself on independence and autonomy, and yet those characteristics are void in the societal belief system regarding the criminal justice system.

When commenting on Foucault's work, the interviewer J.-J. Brochier states, "Your research bears on things that are banal, or which have been made banal because they aren't *seen*. For instance, I find it striking that prisons are in cities and yet *no one sees them*. Or else, if one sees one, one wonders vaguely, whether it's a prison, a school, a barracks, or a hospital. Your book is an important event because it places before our eyes something that no one was previously able to see."

To this, Foucault responded in *Power/Knowledge*, "In a sense that is how history has always been studied. The making visible of what was previously unseen can sometimes be the effect of using a magnifying instrument. . . . But to make visible the unseen can also mean a change of level, addressing oneself to a layer of material which had hitherto had no pertinence for history, and which had not been recognized as having any moral, aesthetic, political or historical power" (Foucault 1980, 50).

This observation is tremendously important to me as it is my life's work and the work of many Native people who are working inside and outside prisons to make the invisible visible! I think as a society we need to acknowledge that locking people up, building prisons where we do not have to see them or can think of them as a possible corporate complex as we drive by, allows us to *not see* or deal with our feelings about prisoners as people. Our society feels "safer" because they are out of our sight and therefore out of our mind, heart, and soul.

HISTORY OF WOMEN'S PRISONS IN THE UNITED STATES

Reading Foucault and examining the contemporary prison systems of Montana and Oregon led to researching the first known prison in the United States that was created to house women. Prior to the opening of the Indiana Reformatory Institute for Women and Girls in Indianapolis, women were housed with men. This was also the first maximum-security female correctional facility in the nation. Rebecca Onion, writing for *Slate*, informs us about the history of Indiana Reformatory Institute for Women and Girls (Onion 2015). The prison was established by two women who were Quaker reformers in response to the allegations of sexual abuse of women prisoners by fellow prisoners and staff at the Indiana State Prison. Onion enlightens us as to the reality of the prison environment versus the skewed historical representation. Quaker women R. Coffin and S. Smith lobbied for the establishment of the facility, and both went on to serve on the board of visitors. The focus was a prioritization of reforming prisoners versus punishment, with the primary task of reintegrating prisoners into the gender roles of Victorian times. Onion quotes the 1876 annual report, which postulates that the mandatory approach implemented was to train the women to "occupy the position assigned to them by God, wives, mothers, and educators of children," while following the rules of the prison. Research on the prison uncovered a history of "mistreatment of the prisoners . . . staff had been accused of humiliation, assault and 'dunking' of prisoners who didn't follow the institution's rules." Solitary confinement, denial of food, denial of medications, physical abuse, and questionable medical experimentation were tools of the system. The lives of Coffin and Smith were not able to live up to the façade of benevolence under the scrutiny of research: Onion highlights that Coffin and Smith resigned after an investigation in 1881 brought to light allegations of abuse such as waterboarding and reports of women stripped naked and put in solitary confinement. More important, under examination, the institution did not live up to its historical reputation of alleged benevolence.

Angela Davis, in *Are Prisons Obsolete?* (2003), calls attention to the fact that even though the experience of women prisoners in the United States has produced a body of literature, small as it might be, the public and even prison activists have been primarily concerned with the experiences of male prisoners. She reminds us that since the end of the eighteenth century, "convicted women have been represented as essentially different from their male counterparts" (65) "with males being labeled as 'social deviants' but yet somehow 'normal' while women are seen as more aberrant and threatening" (66). She asserts that women who committed crimes were subjected to different forms of punishment, such as being put in mental institutions, labeled as deviant women, and viewed as insane. As Davis goes on to state, "gendered as female, this category of insanity was highly sexualized" (67). Furthermore, gendering was an ideological part of the reform movement led by the Quakers, as women prior to reform were viewed as *fallen* women who had transgressed the moral principles tied to womanhood. The reformers felt these women could be saved and, despite the shortcomings of the movement, did change the penal approach to women. The intersection between class and race resulted in white women of means being classified as having mental or emotional disorders, while women of color were classified as criminals.

Once women were housed separately from men, there was a concerted effort to reform them with a focus on domesticity. Davis states, "Architectural changes, domestic regimes, and an all-female custodial staff were implemented in the reformatory program proposed by reformers, and eventually women's prisons became as strongly anchored to the social landscape as men's prisons, but even more invisible. Their greater invisibility was as much of a reflection of the way women's domestic duties under patriarchy were assumed to be normal, natural, and consequentially invisible as it was of the relatively small numbers of women incarcerated in these new institutions" (Davis 2003, 71).

Despite reform efforts to feminize punishment, race and class were and are still part of the equation, as women of color and Native American women were not only segregated from white women—they were often still imprisoned in men's institutions. Of the many tools used to control prisoners, overmedicating them was and still is rampant. To this day psychiatric drugs continue to be prescribed for women prisoners at a much higher rate than for male prisoners (Davis 2003).

Ross informs us that it is crucial to consider and contextualize the concept of female "deviance" as part of the process of criminalization. She states, "The personal experiences of imprisoned women, regardless of race/ethnicity, reflect the structure of the United States in which certain subgroups are not only penalized because of their race/ethnicity (including reservation status), [but] gender and class are controlled as well. This is seen in the violence experienced in prisoners' lives prior to incarceration and in their ultimate criminalization because of their supposed 'deviant' behavior" (Ross 1998, 91). She considers it imperative that research be conducted on the notion of "criminality" by examining the socioeconomic conditions in which crimes happen. When Ross conducted her research, the women's prison was called the Women's Correctional Center (WCC) and was in Deer Lodge, Montana; it is now called the Montana Women's Prison and is in Billings, Montana. When discussing Ross's research, it is referred to as WCC and when discussing the institution in current time it is referred to as MWP. She has found that Native and non-Native women at WCC were imprisoned for crimes ranging from killing abusive family members to writing bad checks for resources to take care of their children. Some women were found guilty of the same offenses as their spouses; they were held responsible by the judge even when their husbands took responsibility for the crimes. Some women pled guilty to save their spouse prison time. Some husbands said their wives were guilty of the crime, while in reality the wives were innocent.

Working with the Native women at CCCF, I found that often a woman would "take the fall" for her significant other, particularly if the significant other was a male. At CCCF, the bulk of the Native women imprisoned are serving time due to crimes related to drugs and alcohol. These crimes range from buying and selling drugs to possession, assault, identify theft, and robbery. There are many cases where the woman is an accessory to the crime, from driving a get-away vehicle to holding the drugs for her significant other, but she ends up with the same sentence, a longer sentence, or a sentence for a crime that she did not commit. Relationships, past abuse, current domestic violence, addiction, socioeconomic situation, and lack of resources are often the foundation for the crimes committed. Ross (1998) reminds readers that "being in prison does not equate with guilt" (90).

NARRATIVES FROM NATIVE AMERICAN WOMEN'S EXPERIENCE OF INCARCERATION

While we may not currently have access to or knowledge of the historical experience of Native American women in the early penal institutions throughout the United States, we do have contemporary personal stories that have been shared. Ross (1998) shares narratives of experiences of women in prison at WCC in Montana. The experiences of these Native women reflect the issues of power and control, racism, stereotyping, faulty rehabilitation programs, prison subcultures, incarcerated mothers, and lack of meaningful cultural programs. It is important to note that Ross contends that women experience prison differently than men and that Native women at WCC experienced prison differently than white women. Some of those differences are due to the following factors:

There were not trained staff who are knowledgeable about Native American culture.

Native American inmates who ask for culture-specific programs are labeled as troublemakers and may suffer ill treatment by staff and guards.

There are few spiritual support services for Native American women, while there are numerous faith-based groups serving non-Native women.

Native American women are not allowed to sing songs or pray in their Native languages unless it is a sanctioned activity because it makes the guards nervous. The non-Native women are allowed to sign hymns and pray together outside of regular church services.

Prison staff and guards often stereotype the belief system of Native American women.

Native American women's sacred items are not treated respectfully while the bibles and communion accoutrements of those who practice other faiths are treated reverently.

Additionally, Ross asserts that Native women, who are disproportionately housed in the maximum-security unit, experience prison differently than those in the general population. She contends that the environment at WCC is extremely homophobic, making it extremely difficult for lesbian prisoners. I would add that since writing the book in 1998, Ross would undoubtedly find that prisoners who identify as lesbian, gay, bisexual, or transgender experience MWP as a place that is still homophobic. Ross describes the conditions at WCC during her research period as extremely deficient, from the condition of the facility to the medical care, treatment programs, and rehabilitative programs that have a focus on control.

Ross (1998) shares experiences of Native American women inmates under several categories. The first is the assessment process, where they describe being told to strip naked; being searched with a focus on their body cavities, often defined as sexual assault and rape; and being forced to shower in front of one or more guards while being deloused. Once given a gown they are put into a lockdown room for a period of fourteen days. During the lockdown period, they are photographed and given their prison identification number. She quotes Faith (1993), who states that "part of the 'ceremony' of assessment is to break a prisoner's spirit and ready her for rehabilitation" (as cited in Ross 1988, 151). As Native American women, they find that this type of "ceremony" has no equivalent in traditional restorative justice.

Medical care is described as inadequate, and that is typical of women's prisons. Treatments are described as painful, often overlooked when needed, performed when not necessary, and humiliating (Ross 1988). There is no understanding or acceptance of cultural norms for Native American women when it comes to illness. In Native culture we do not leave our loved ones alone when they are hospitalized. Rather, friends, family, spiritual leaders, and community members gather to pray and offer support to the ill person and family. Most often the corrections system does not allow family to see their hospitalized loved one because the family member is still an inmate and under the control of the system. Currently the process at MWP does not include exceptions (i.e., long-term or critically ill offenders); and all visitors fill out the same request form and must follow the outlined polices (Montana Women's Prison 2022).

As discussed earlier, the corrections system uses medication as a form of control. Many women enter prison without addiction problems but exit addicted to narcotic drugs. In addition, women who enter prison with drug addiction do not receive adequate treatment for their drug addiction but rather go through withdrawal while also being introduced to new mind-altering drugs. The purpose of "breaking" the spirit of prisoners using these dehumanizing tactics is to create a "model" prisoner class. These "model" prisoners will then become submissive to corrections staff. The tactic of medicating the poor can be found throughout the world of public social services in the United States and beyond. Employing these methods can have lasting effects on the women, furthering their addictions and medical conditions (Davis 2003). The general public would be shocked to know that being incarcerated does not mean that prisoners do not have access to alcohol and drugs.

In her discussion of education programs for prisoners, Ross (1998) asserts that prison staff focus on rehabilitation with an emphasis on conformity. She also asserts that the type of training the women receive is based upon Euro-American culture with the focus on turning out wives, mothers, and homemakers, disregarding the fact that there is a major percentage of women in prison who are already mothers and who are also heads of households. The majority of Native American women in prison are mothers and also the primary provider for their family.

At the time Ross (1998) was conducting her research, prisoners at WCC had access to three levels of educational classes: college courses, remedial adult education for those with either a high school diploma or GED test below a high-school level, and GED preparation. Those classified with a "closed" status were not allowed access to any education programs. It is important to note that just because educational courses were offered does not mean that access was easy, that corrections staff were supportive, or that women had access to the materials and support they needed to be academically successful. Today, the MWP only offers classes to obtain high school equivalency diplomas; college preparation classes; and courses to learn computer, personal, and job-related skills. There is no opportunity to take college courses or to earn a college degree. A woman's ability to participate in any program, vocational or academic, is determined by her status, which includes the determination by the system of her security level and her privilege group while she is incarcerated. Her status can change while she is in prison, as determined by Department of Corrections staff.

Ross (1998) details the training opportunities for women at the time of her research, which were minimal compared to training opportunities offered to male inmates. This remains true today. As previously discussed, participation in a vocational program is dependent upon the inmate's classification. Inmates who are not allowed access to the programs are those who have a "closed" status, which is when "in locked housing due to ongoing or serious behavior management problems," or who have any level other than "satisfactory" and are housed in the general population (Montana Women's Prison 2022). Furthermore, there are not enough openings for the programs that do exist.

Racism is evident and prevalent. Native women prisoners assert that white women receive the best in-house positions, while Native women are relegated to the lowest-paying menial jobs, such as working in the kitchen, laundry, and maintenance. Ross (1998) asserts that this type of work cannot be considered "training" but rather is another form of structural racism that continues the efforts of colonization and gendering. Colonialism brought to the United States and Canada the very elements Foucault (1977) discussed, where the inmate is reduced to classification and manipulation by the prison industrial complex. Prior to contact on the lands now called the United States and Canada, there were no jails or prisons!

The counseling and treatment programs at WCC during the time of Ross's (1998) research are described as focusing on building inmate self-esteem. The inmates express that in reality, their self-esteem is lowered due to the disrespectful way they are treated by the staff. One Native woman prisoner who became an outspoken advocate for culturally specific programming was labeled a troublemaker. Ross asserts that the counseling model focuses on individual deficiencies and building self-esteem while ignoring the "social structure, society's deficiencies, or the effects of the prison regime on prisoners' mental health" (1998, 134).

Early women prisoners experienced an emphasis on religion as part of the rehabilitation process. Ross (1998) contends that WCC follows the same philosophy. She shares the mission statement of one fellowship program, the White Harvest Jail/Prison Ministry and Transition Program, which states, "Prisoners are encouraged to participate in courses that instruct in American patriotism, citizenship, community relationships, responsibilities and obligations" (135). The organization published a narrative from an ex-prisoner named Linda. Linda describes herself as a drug addict, an alcoholic, a liar, a thief, and an immoral person. After attending a service where national songs were sung, the Pledge of Allegiance was said, and thanks were given to God, Linda escaped from the "Serpent's Spells, Snares and Shambles." Linda began reading about U.S. history and was moved by the signers of the Declaration of Independence, gained knowledge about wars, and learned of the price the Founding Fathers paid to obtain freedom and Christian Americanism. While Linda's experience is certainly valid to her, it does not ring true for many Native Americans. The mythical and romanticized version of not only the founding of this country but also the Native American experience of colonization is painful for many of us Native Americans. There is historical evidence for the motivation of prison and its programs to convert prisoners to a Judeo-Christian belief system (see, for example, Onion's article "The Pen" [2015]), and these same processes can be found in contemporary times.

Fortunately, since the passage of the American Indian Religious Freedom Act in 1978, Native American prisoners can no longer legally be denied the right to practice their spirituality. However, enforcement of the act does not happen in every state, prison, or jail. Since the publishing of Ross's book in 1998, MWP has built a sweat lodge for Native American women inmates. The Native women inmates felt it would be beneficial both to the inmates and the institution if there were a Native counselor as well as culturally specific treatment programs. Governor

Stan Stephens, Montana's governor at that time, responded to the request from Native prisoners that he would implement such requests if the tribes of Montana helped to fund the requested positions (Ross 1998). Ross (1998) clarifies the neocolonial racism of the attitude of the governor, as white communities are not asked to finance white counselors who work at the prisons. I must add that the pathway for white Judeo-Christian spiritual leaders has only one barrier: the ability to pass a background check. Meanwhile, Native American spiritual leaders are often turned away for unknown reasons.

Ross (1998) informs us that in 1991 the Native women prisoners received permission to establish a Native women's group. The women viewed this hour each Sunday as part of their rehabilitation and survival, and an opportunity to engage in spiritual ceremony. Conversely, the prison classified the time as "recreation." Eventually the Native women could burn sweetgrass if they resided in the general population. Once again their status comes into the equation of provision of services. The staff, however, did not like having to allow them to do so as they thought it might be a drug, and to them it smelled like marijuana. It is important to note that white women confined to maximum security or segregation had full access to their religious practices, while Native women in the same statuses were not allowed to smudge with sweetgrass.

The prohibition of religious freedom for Native inmates at WCC, according to Ross (1998), was problematic on many levels:

The denial of religious freedom was and is illegal.
Native men prisoners in Montana were permitted to practice the sweat lodge ceremony.
White women prisoners had unfettered access to their religious practices.
Native American spirituality is not viewed by prison staff as credible.

Native American spirituality including the sweat lodge ceremony and smudging have helped Native people including prisoners heal from and survive the brutality of colonization and incarceration. The prison system punishes Native women for the crimes they commit, and by neglecting to provide access to or respect for their spiritual practices and beliefs, they are punished not only in body but also in the soul. The classification by status within the prison system is discussed by Ross (1998), who points out that Euro-American society discourages women from expressing anger. When women in prison express anger, often by acts of resistance, often they are sent to maximum security and classified as "unmanageable."

The Native American women prisoners in the Healing the Sacred Hoop workshop were classified as "incorrigible." Many of them had been in segregation more than once. Ross (1998) describes women housed in maximum security or segregation as women who have been pushed emotionally, are angry, and are extremely vulnerable; Native women are disproportionally represented. She describes the act of confinement coupled with isolation as being especially difficult as the women are not allowed visits, cannot participate in programs or religious services, and have little daily time outside their cells. These "unmanageable" or "incorrigible" women are often those with the highest need of services. Often being confined brings flashbacks of prior abuse, and many Native women have post–traumatic stress disorder (Ross 1998).

While progress has been made since the passage of the American Indian Religious Freedom Act, that does not mean that further accommodations do not need to be made; it does not mean the spiritual (religious) rights of Native American prisoners are upheld. Beran (2005), in an article titled "Native Americans in Prison: The Struggle for Religious Freedom," writes that while the Nebraska State Penitentiary has allowed for a greater expression of Native identity after a class action lawsuit was filed, there are still grievances. At CCCF some of those grievances stem from the eligibility requirements for spiritual activities. Another grievance arising in Oregon is the denial of requests for family members of inmates to participate in special ceremonies, which is both racist and an insult to culture. Religion and the practice of it in this country are not only seen as a family affair; the prison system itself was designed to promote a Christian-Judaic sense of values and morals. It is counterproductive to exclude the families of Native American inmates from participating in special spiritual events such as the yearly First Foods Feast. Beran asserts, "One of the steps ultimately required to achieve religious equity for Native Americans will be the allowance and encouragement of Native religious practice and spiritual observance in prisons" (Beran 2005, 54). Beran understands that extended family and community support networks are at the center of Native life as part of our culture and society.

As discussed earlier, a large proportion of Native women are victims of sexual abuse in their childhood and as adults. The prison system does not protect women from further sexual abuse. Ross (1998) contends that homophobia is part of Montana's societal thinking, and that thinking is evident inside the prison, among both staff and inmates. She informs us that in 1995 Montana proposed a bill that would have classified gay adults as "violent felons." They were often called abnormal, sick, and not fit to have children.

TWO SPIRITED WOMEN

At WCC as well as CCCF, women, both Native and non-Native, are often involved in what Ross (1998) terms "situational" lesbian relationships. Women of course long for relationship, companionship, connection, and love whether they are in or out of prison. It is not unfathomable that women would seek out each other for a relationship while in prison. Ross describes the staff at the WCC as viewing lesbian relationships as creating dangerous situations and causing tension and disruption among the prisoners. Ross cites the dominant societal view of same-sex relationships as "sinful," "deviant," and "sick," with inmates at WCC employing the remedies of "counseling," "medication," and increased time in segregation for those prisoners in same-sex relationships.

Everton Bailey Jr. reported in the *Oregonian* that Circuit Judge J. Burdette Pratt in Umatilla County had ordered the State of Oregon to house a transgender female inmate in a cell separate from male inmates and to protect her from harassment (Bailey 2019). The inmate, Brandy Hall, is a woman in a male prison and is thought to be the first in Oregon at a men's prison. Hall's attorney, Tara Herivel, stated that the court decision "paves the way for other transgender inmates to make the same request unless the Oregon Department of Corrections creates an overarching housing policy for transgender and intersex prisoners" (Bailey 2019).

At CCCF one of the chaplains is a lesbian woman who is married to her partner, and she gave birth to their son during the time I conducted the Healing the Sacred Hoop workshop. Of course, this example is more current than those from Ross's (1998) research. Almost all Native American tribes have historically embraced gay, lesbian, bisexual, or transgendered tribal members and did not marginalize them. D. Brayboy (Tosneoc Tuscarora) writes about gender roles that existed among Native people at first contact:

> At the point of contact, all Native American societies acknowledged three to five gender roles: Female, male, Two Spirit female, Two Spirit male and transgendered. LGBT Native Americans wanting to be identified within their respective tribes and not grouped with other races officially adopted the term "Two Spirit" from the Ojibwe language in Winnipeg, Manitoba, 1989. Each tribe has their own specific term, but there was a need for a universal term that the general population could understand. The Navajo refer to Two Spirits as Nádleehí (one who is transformed), among the Lakota is Winkté (indicative of a male who has a compulsion to behave as a female), Niizh Manidoowag (two spirit) in Ojibwe, Hemaneh (half man, half woman) in Cheyenne, to name a few. As the purpose of *Two Spirit* is to be used as a universal term in the English language, it is not always translatable with the same meaning in Native languages. For example, in the Iroquois Cherokee language, there is no way to translate the term, but the Cherokee do have gender variance terms for "women who feel like men" and vice versa. (Brayboy 2016)

These gender variances were considered sinful, deviant, and dangerous by colonizers, and hence came the effort to eliminate such gender roles and to conform to the binary prescribed two gender roles of the Judeo-Christian belief system.

Writing in the *Washington Post*, Katherine Davis-Young describes Arizona's first Two Spirit Powwow celebrating LGBTQ Native Americans: "The sound of drums, singing and prayers marked the opening of a powwow in Phoenix on a Saturday afternoon this month. Marchers carried the flags of the United States and some of Arizona's tribal nations onto the grass field, but the procession also included rainbow flags, and the pink and blue transgender flag" (Davis-Young 2019). Colonization and assimilation sought to erase customs, oral traditions, belief systems, and spiritual practices of gender and were unable to understand that these things are not tied to sexuality. There is a growing movement to return to Native American traditions that historically recognized more than two genders. Zachary Pullin (Chippewa Cree) describes his experience growing up on our reservation, Rocky Boy, as a Two Spirit, meaning a Native LGBTQ person: "I never entered the dance arena with confidence like the male grass Plains traditional and fancy dancers at grand entry. I had grown up with the idea in my own mind that I was less of a man, and also, being both physically and characteristically different, I felt vulnerable in expressing myself in those circles. Even if the notion was all in my head, there was a deep sense that I couldn't present my whole self in that space" (Pullin 2016). After Pullin attended a Two Spirit gathering that brought together Two Spirit people customs, including traditional dancing and storytelling, he felt authentic entering the dance arena, and that he had found his place and identity in the circle.

On a visit home, the concept of two-spiritedness was one of many subjects that I discussed with my female Elders. They advised me that for Cree people, Two Spirited people were loved and respected because they are our people and members of our families and tribe. Two Spirited people were often thought to have a connection to the mystical and spiritual that others, except for Medicine People, did not have and were therefore held in high esteem. Pullin cites author Sabine Lang, who in the book *Men as Women, Women as Men: Changing Gender in Native American Culture*, articulates that in many tribes, Two Spirit people were historically "keepers of traditions, tellers of the stories of creation, and healers" (Pullin 2016).

RACISM AND THE SYSTEM

The issues of racism and the treatment of prisoners by prison staff are discussed by Ross with her contention that at WCC, Native women were viewed in a negative manner by some prison staff because of their race or ethnicity. She cites an experience of telling a staff member that she wanted to interview a Native inmate. The staff member responded that the Native woman was a good candidate for the study because she represented "everything bad in Indian culture" (Ross 1998, 46), yet the staff member never portrayed any white inmates or white culture in a negative manner. Women in the study described negative treatment they received because they were Native. This treatment included harassment; being labeled as "troublemakers" or having "behavioral problems"; being penalized for speaking out for cultural and spiritual needs, sometimes through being classified as "unmanageable"; and being sent to segregation for long periods of time where they were not allowed to participate in cultural or spiritual events.

CCCF used moving Native inmates to segregation as an act of denial of the spiritual services. Prison staff used it as a tool of power and control. The Native women were allowed one large-scale event per year. The First Foods Feast is something that the women look forward to all year long. They put a great deal of work into making giveaway items for their guests. Organized by Red Lodge, the event celebrates the first foods that are sacred and traditional to tribal people of the Northwest. Red Lodge gathers food donations from many of the nine tribes of Oregon. These foods often include elk, deer, salmon, huckleberries, a variety of roots, and fry bread. Elders and Medicine People from the Longhouse of the Warm Springs Tribe travel to lead the services. Drummers and flute players, along with storytellers, join in with community members from many different tribes. It is a day of joy, renewal, and connection to culture, Creator, and the Ancestors. Unfortunately, the prison staff have used it as a tool of condign power to threaten the women, telling them they better behave or they will not be allowed to attend because they will either be confined to their quarters or in segregation. For several years we saw a trend of Native women being placed in segregation just prior to the First Foods Feast as a punishment for slight or invented transgressions.

SEXUAL INTIMIDATION AND ASSAULT IN PRISON

Ross (1998) brings to light another tool of control that women in prison, both non-Native and Native, have experienced: that of sexual intimidation. Ross (1998) imparts some of the experiences that Native women at WCC shared with her, which range from being spied on when dressing or undressing to being raped. Ross reminds us that the rape of Native women has been happening since colonization.

There have been many reported instances of rape at CCCF involving both Native and non-Native women. Numerous lawsuits have been filed in the last few years alleging rape and sexual assault by prison guards, maintenance staff, contractors, and the prison doctor. In some of the cases drugs or other contraband items were exchanged for sexual acts (*Prison Legal News*, 2013). Even if contraband was exchanged, because of the power held by the contraband provider, these sexual acts are not consensual. Many women inmates have mental health problems, are addicts, and have suffered from being sexually assaulted in their lives from childhood onward. These women are vulnerable and, in many ways, powerless.

It is essential that we are also aware of and accept the reality that women in prison experience sexual assault by other prisoners. Piecora found that "the rate is at least 3 times higher for females (13.7%) than males (4.2%). This has been attributed to the fact that many prison officials do not view female-on-female sexual assault as 'true rape,' making them less likely to reprimand inmates. Furthermore, as the female prison population has grown at a dramatic rate, states have been unable to keep up. Therefore, female prison facilities tend to be overcrowded and poorly designed, making them difficult to police" (*Jurist* 2014). The reasons behind why female-on-female sexual assault takes place among women prisoners are many. Robert Dumond found:

> Contrary to popular perception, it must be understood that no inmate is immune from sexual victimization. This being said, certain groups of inmates appear to be more vulnerable. They include (a) young, inexperienced; (b) physically small or weak; (c) inmates suffering from mental illness and/or developmental disabilities; (d) middle-class, not "tough" or "streetwise"; (e) not gang affiliated; (f) known to be homosexual or overtly effeminate (if male); (g) convicted of sexual crimes; (h) violated the "code of silence" or "rats"; (i) disliked by staff/other inmates; (j) previously sexually assaulted. . . . The issue of race has also been identified . . . especially in those settings with disproportionate racial populations and high racial tension. (Dumond 2000, 408–9)

While there are no studies on why a Native woman prisoner would sexually assault another female prisoner, Native or non-Native, certainly their own victimization may be a contributing factor. The American Civil Liberties Union states that "the vast majority of women in prison have been victims of violence prior to their incarceration including domestic violence, rape, sexual assault and child abuse" (ACLU 2017). Prior experience as victims of violence and sexual assault as well as their own previous sexual and violent behavior are factors to be considered.

MOTHERS BEHIND BARS

It is impossible to consider the life of women behind bars without discussing those who are imprisoned mothers. The American Civil Liberties Union found that an estimated 700,000 state and federal prisoners were parents to nearly 1.5 million children under age eighteen (ACLU 2017). The U.S. Department of Justice (2010) in a special report on statistics found that the number of parents of minor children held in the nation's prisons increased by 79 percent between 1991 and midyear 2007 (1). While I was not able to find specific statistics on the number of Native American women prisoners who are mothers, Red Lodge estimates that "the majority of Native women in prison have children under the age of eighteen" (Red Lodge, n.d.).

Ross (1998) describes the cultural aspects that are unique to Native American mothers in prison. She reminds us that the sense of family and family structure is different in Native culture than in Western culture. For Native women who have grown up within the culture and particularly with close ties to reservations and family, the structure is one of extended family life. Grandparents, aunts, uncles, and siblings all play a role in family life. She states that "when this family structure is functioning, members of the extended family are responsible to and for one another" (Ross 1998, 197). It is uncommon in a Native home not to have an aunty, uncle, cousin, or grandparent either living in the home or dividing time among the family. I can remember my grandfather George Denny coming to stay with us. He had his own home and a wife, but he liked to stay with his children from time to time, especially if he and his wife weren't getting along. In Native culture, an Elder need not ask permission to stay, and Elders are always welcomed. One would never think of asking them how long they plan to stay; when they are ready, they move on. When

Grandpa George was with us, he was in charge. By the time I was three years old, I was put on a chair to wash the family dishes (when we had food). I was to see after the other children, even those that were older than me. My role as the oldest girl was defined and special to me. Family power is much different than in the individualistic Western culture where parents exert their rights over everyone else. A good example is that in Western culture, people are not allowed to discipline someone else's child unless given explicit permission, and the concept of "my child" and "my rules" is the norm. In Native families children receive love, support, and redirection from all family members who are their Elders. If a parent or primary caretaker is removed from the family, as in the case of being imprisoned, there is a circle of support for children that is flexible.

It is critical to note the distinction that Ross (1998) makes between reservation and non-reservation functioning families. She stresses that Native women with close ties to reservation and family tend to place their children with extended family and that the mother is satisfied with the placement; Native women without close ties to reservation and family tend to have their children placed in the foster care system. Despite the Indian Child Welfare Act (ICWA) of 1978, a federal law that is designed to place American Indian children with American Indian families, the courts, social service agencies, and tribes have not been successful in ensuring that the law is being followed. Ross contends that non-reservation Native women entering prison are less aware of their rights under ICWA and, because they do not have tribal connections and relationships, they do not have the legal support that reservation Natives have in where their children are placed.

As one can imagine, Native mothers in prison suffer emotionally when separated from their children. They miss them and desire to see them. They also feel guilt that they are away from them due to being incarcerated. The traditional role of mothers is described by Janine Pease (Crow-Hidatsa) as follows: "American Indian women were the essential keepers of culture, language, worldview, rituals, and practices; in essence the purveyors of beliefs and behaviors" (as cited in Fitzgerald and Fitzgerald 2005, xv).

In the Healing the Sacred Hoops workshop, the women delved into many painful subjects. One of the most painful for the women was dealing with the family life and parenting of their children. Many of the women in the workshop would come to terms with and discuss the physical and emotional abuse their children suffered from themselves, their co-parent, or the extended family. Visitation, parenting programs, and programs that allow incarcerated moms to interact with their children vary from institution to institution.

Ross (1998) sees the visitation system at WCC as being another tool of power and control that targets Natives unfairly in comparison to white inmates, and those sentiments hold true at CCCF. Native inmates have specific barriers to seeing their children as well as other visitors. These barriers include the following:

Many families are far away in distance from the prison facility.

Not all women are imprisoned in their own state.

Many families cannot afford to travel to visit.

Children are placed in foster homes that are non-Native and may have foster parents who are unwilling to bring the children to visit; the foster care system does not require them to do so.

Visitation requires that the adult bringing a child must be able to pass a background check, which the placement person might not be able to pass.

The women need to see their children and the children need to see their mothers. The system can be more flexible and provide better access by offering innovative programs for mothers behind bars. The system can be more collaborative with social service programs, tribes, and court-appointed advocates to foster visitation between mothers and children.

It is impossible for any of us who have not experienced incarceration to fathom completely the life of someone behind bars. In addition, the prison industrial complex is complicated, and it is not accessible to those seeking to understand its workings. It is easy for any citizen never to consider the beginnings, philosophical underpinnings, goals, and culture of the systems of incarceration. I hope the work of many, including myself, who strive to make the invisible visible will enlighten others, soften people's hearts and minds, and spur change.

CHAPTER 4

Historical Trauma and the Need for Healing and Perspectives of Native Spirituality

Maria Yellow Horse Brave Heart (Hunkpapa-Oglala Lakota) defines historical trauma as the cumulative emotional and psychological wounding over the lifespan and across generations, emanating from massive group trauma (Brave Heart 1999). Historical unresolved grief is the grief that accompanies the trauma. For more than twenty-five years, first as a clinical social worker and more recently as a clinical researcher, she has investigated generational trauma and its impact. She asserts that for more than five hundred years, Native Americans have suffered physical, emotional, social, and spiritual genocide from European and American colonialist policies and actions.

Contemporary Native American people are not faring well, and our people, as individuals and as communities, need to heal from the historical unresolved grief. The effects of historical trauma include unsettled emotional trauma, depression, high mortality rates, high rates of alcohol and drug abuse, significant problems of child abuse, domestic violence, rising rates of suicide, and over-representation in the criminal justice system (Brave Heart 1999). Racism, oppression, and internalized oppression exacerbate these destructive behaviors. One generation's trauma has an impact on subsequent generations. Our souls are wounded.

In 2015 delegates attending the thirty-third annual National Indian Child Welfare Association conference, Protecting Our Children, heard keynote speaker Dr. Brave Heart consider the tenets of gentle action theory in contrast to traditional ways in the provision of healing to Native women's experiences of incarceration. She asserted that "the most effective healing methods for Native people must emerge from within tribal communities and must draw on traditional ways of knowing and being including spirituality" (Brave Heart 2015). Her words raised the possibility of gentle action theory and traditional ways working in a corresponding manner.

Eduardo Duran (Navajo-Apache) discusses the need for a new method of treating Native peoples using a concept he terms "liberation psychology through hybridism," which addresses some of the underlying issues Native American patients experience that lead them to seek counseling (Duran 2006, 13). Trauma passed down from generation to generation resulting in internalized oppression, combined with centuries of colonizing processes, affects Native peoples at a soul-deep level.

Duran (2006) introduced a healing process that restores humanity in such a manner that it is in harmony with natural laws. He asserts that culture is a part of the soul, that we are not separate from culture; when that culture is one of oppression, we are wounded and need to be liberated from that oppression in order to heal.

Duran (2006) asserts that the mental health professions have perpetuated psychological oppression ever since the earliest days when the Catholic Church gained power in Indian Country, imposing the will and strategies of colonizing institutions and implementing paradigms that clash with Native values, beliefs, and traditional ways of being. He believes that healing can only come by addressing the historical soul-deep wounds that resulted from the past and current oppression of Native people. Without ways to heal, our descendants will continue to experience a variety of psychic and spiritual sufferings.

Duran explains that liberation psychology through hybridism requires that "cross-cultural" and "cultural sensitivity" must be transcended "to think or see the truth in more than one way" (2006, 14). He defines "epistemological hybridism" as acknowledging and validating the actual life-world experience of a person or group as their core truth simply because that is what it is. For too long there has been a need in his profession to validate ways of knowing based on Western empiricism. By acknowledging and validating results in a liberating psychology, he asserts, this decolonizing of patients will prevent future chronic problems. Duran contends that this decolonization process applies not only to Native Americans or people of color but also to members of the dominant Western society. The larger dominant society has also been conditioned by the processes of colonization; therefore, decolonization is an act of coming against what has been imposed on them. Healing and the restoration of humanity can be done in a harmonious way for all members of society.

Both Brave Heart (2000) and Duran (2006) discuss the ramifications of colonization and the connection to trauma, to unresolved grief that has resulted in loss of culture and identity, and in alcoholism, poverty, and despair. Incarceration is another consequence of colonization and historical trauma, and it is on the rise in Indian Country.

In an article in the *Calgary Journal* Karina Zapata discusses the role that oppression plays in the mental health of people of color, including Indigenous people (Zapata 2020). She advocates for the decolonization of mental health. She shares that there are professionals across this continent who are "working to decolonize mental health by working toward collective healing to salve the wounds of colonization and oppression-based trauma, guided by Indigenous decolonial work" (Zapata 2020). Three of those professionals who are working toward decolonizing mental health throughout Canada and the United States are Elisa Lacerda-Vandenborn, Mimi Khúc, and Jennifer Mullan.

Mullan states, "We do a lot of ancestral work, a lot of intergenerational trauma work, dealing with rage as a function and a normal understanding system of living in a world that continues to oppress us and not provide many of us with what we need." She further states, "Decolonization is not a metaphor and trying to be better mental health advocates is not going to be enough. Being culturally competent, in my humble, loving opinion, is not enough" (quoted in Zapata 2020).

Khúc describes how she suffered from extreme postpartum depression, was unable to find culturally specific resources, and realized that the individualistic and medical approach she was experiencing in living in the United States was not meeting her needs. She used her own expertise in Asian American studies to find answers on her own and was able to recognize the many underlying narratives that are part of her life. These include "the difficulty of belonging as an Asian American in North America, her family's refugee background and the pressures of being an Asian American mother." She continues, "When I say decolonizing, I want to question and interrogate the ways that these larger forces and institutions have told us what counts as mental health and what counts as suffering. In order to interrogate that, I have to draw on community and think about the kinds of knowledge that come out of our own communities around what suffering is" (quoted in Zapata 2020).

Lacerda-Vandenborn, who moved to Canada from Brazil, found herself experiencing severe bouts of loneliness and depression. Her visit to a therapist left her both struggling and blaming herself. On her own she realized that missing her family and a sense of community, which were core to her life in Brazil, was what was causing the depression and loneliness. She asserts that "many oppressed individuals need connection, which the current mental health system doesn't make space for. It is our time to participate in decolonization. This is a shared process" (quoted in Zapata 2020).

While it may be difficult for people to recognize trauma caused by colonization and oppression as a mental health issue, Mullan informs us that it is often rooted in colonization and opression: "I feel like so much of the depression, of the anxiety, of the constant state of trauma that we are going through, this complex, developmental trauma, this concept of 'fight, flight, and, freeze' response that we're in are due to systems of oppression—are due to these overt and covert acts of racism and colonization and the effects of colonization on our minds, bodies and spirits" (quoted in Zapata 2020). She echoes the perspectives of Brave Heart (2000) and Duran (2006) that suffering or trauma is caused by oppression and is often passed down through generations.

Zapata cites a 2018 study published in *World Psychiatry* in which scientists suggest: "Trauma can be passed down to subsequent generations through an enduring change in the function of DNA. This change is epigenetic, as opposed to genetic. That means the structure of the DNA itself isn't changed, but the expression of the DNA is. This can have a lasting effect on the individual and their offspring." Khúc says, "So to decolonize the system is to take a practice related to Indigenous decolonial projects but is also separate from it." Lacerda-Vandenborn describes this as a *"third space,* which sits in between Western perspectives and Indigenous perspectives." For Khúc and Lacerda-Vandenborn this space between Western perspectives and Indigenous perspectives allows for the integration from all three perspectives providing people what they need for mental health and is critical for the process decolonizing the provision of mental health services.

Terry Cross (Seneca Nation) provides a Native American perspective on spirituality and mental health (Cross 2002). Cross advises us that "while specific teachings and beliefs vary among Indian Peoples, there is an almost universal belief in the importance of spirituality and the influence of spiritual forces in the balance of one's life" (22). He explicates Indian beliefs that we consider ourselves spirits, spirits that are on a human journey in this world. The journey is one of complexity between the physical world in which our bodies dwell and our mental processes, which include our thoughts and emotions. We view our environment in a holistic manner and include not just the physical; it is important to us, but the environment also encompasses our family and our culture as well as the animate and inanimate. Spiritual forces are of great significance. Cross explains that "the spiritual forces outside of us and the spiritual learned practices that become part of us" form our relational world view (22).

Cross clarifies his view of spirituality as being more than religion and rather as the power of the human spirit. He elucidates the concept of spirituality: "It is the complex and often conflicting nature of spiritual teachings, a sense of purpose and being, a sense of future, a sense of a higher power guiding and shaping our existence. It is a sense of seeking understanding of the mystery of human existence. . . . This world view, in which well-being is balanced between mind, body, spirit, and context, teaches that these elements of life have equal weight; achieving balance among these various functions is in essence the objective of our human existence" (Cross 2002, 22). Cross cites the need to understand mental health from more than a biochemical, personality, or functioning point of view but rather to understand the Native American perspective when working with Native American clients. Cross emphasizes that American Indians have always known and embraced spirituality as part of the healing process. Ritual, ceremony, and spiritual interventions are part of our healing practices.

BRANDIE (KLAMATH-MODOC)

Brandie and I first met when she was incarcerated at the Coffee Creek Correctional Facility. She was in her first stint at Coffee Creek and I would go on to be a mentor to her when she got out. Brandie would return to CCCF. Brandie has graciously chosen to share her some of her story.

The first time I was in prison I was twenty-four years old and I didn't understand the impact I was making on my life. I was prideful about the crimes that I had committed (assault). I stabbed a woman while drunk at a party. Because I'd never been in trouble for major offenses, I got a plea deal and the DA dropped the Measure 11 charges. I remember a month after intake I was placed in G unit, the dayroom had closed for the night, and as I stood in the doorway of my cell and heard all 60-something doors close, reality hit me. I think I adapted fairly quickly. I had family inside that took me under their wing. I started working at the DMV call center and made friends with other Native women. Prison wasn't that bad. I worked a 9-to-5 job, hung out with friends and gained a lot of weight. I went through the AIP treatment program, Turning Point, and was released one-and-a-half years early. Because of my belief "prison wasn't that bad" I think that's why I went back. I honestly just went through the motions.

The second time I went to CCCF was in 2015. I was a mess. My drug use and alcohol use were at an all-time high. I had lost my sister and my dad in 2012, my kids were teenagers and were used to me not being around, I was angry, hurt, felt sorry for myself, mildly suicidal, and I was tired. I asked to be revoked. I knew I needed to sit down. This time of incarceration, I stayed to myself. I didn't care about reuniting with people I knew on the inside, I didn't talk to anyone, I didn't want friends. I got on the stair stepper and I stepped out my anger, I walked around and around the track until I wore out the soles in my prison-issued shoes several times. I thought about my family, I thought about how I felt ashamed, I thought about how time escaped me and my children were almost adults now, I thought about how I was going to correct this, I thought about how I grew to hate myself, I thought about how I wanted to feel human again. I wanted a clean slate. I once again got accepted into the Turning Point program which focuses on cognitive behavioral therapy and I stripped away all of my know-it-all BS and admitted that I didn't know shit about how to become somebody different. I became teachable at that moment and was willing to listen and to learn and to look at things with a new perspective. I made a decision that I didn't want to kill myself, I wanted my family back, I wanted to quit drinking and drugs once and for all. I was so focused on myself I didn't have the time or urge to participate in my surroundings. I worked my job at the canteen distribution center, which is a good opportunity for women. I ate, slept, and repeated. I called home on Saturday morning and talked to my mom and that was my life.

Later on, we will return to Brandie's story.

CONSIDERATIONS FOR THE MENTAL HEALTH OF NATIVE AMERICAN WOMEN IN CCCF

As leader of the Healing the Sacred Hoop project for Native American women incarcerated at CCCF, I focused on the emotional healing of the women in the group. No one involved with the project is a therapist or psychologist; rather are all spiritual leaders and guides. The ceremonies and rituals that include spiritual interventions are needed and longed for by the women who participate in the program. None of the women served would argue that any woman in prison is mentally healthy. Prison is not a place where it is easy to stay mentally healthy if you arrive in that manner. In addition, the life experiences, decisions, and actions that bring a woman to prison are not those of a person who is emotionally healthy or balanced. All women who are incarcerated need mental health services. There are cultural differences in terms of mental health services when working with Native people.

The American Psychiatric Association (2010) provides a fact sheet that details several cultural differences for American Indian and Alaska Native community members seeking mental health services. These cultural differences are considered norms. They include:

"A historical distrust of the outside population exists among many American Indian communities. Individuals tend to have negative opinions of non-Indian health service providers, and traditional healing is used by a majority of Native Americans" (comment by H. Meredith, March 2, 2016, on American Indians / Alaskan Natives [blog forum, 2016]).

"The words 'depressed' and 'anxious' are absent from some American Indian and Alaska Native languages" (Meredith 2016).

A culturally "different expression of illness such as ghost sickness and heartbreak syndrome, do not correspond to *The Diagnostic and Statistical Manual of Mental Disorders* (DSM) diagnoses" (Meredith 2016).

"In the Northern Plains study, 61% of the children had experienced a traumatic event" (Meredith 2016).

The American Indian and Alaska Native population report higher rates of frequent distress than the general population.

High prevalence of substance abuse and alcohol dependence is tied to a high risk for concurrent mental health problems.

Alcohol abuse is a problem for a substantial portion of the American Indian adult population, but widely varies among different tribes.

The prevalence of suicide is a strong indication of the necessity of mental health services in the American Indian / Alaska Native (AI/AN) community (American Psychiatric Association 2010).

The National Alliance on Mental Illness (NAMI) held a symposium in 2003 announcing the release of a new resource manual. According to the press release, Cynthia Mala, PhD (Dakotah), noted that the "Power of the World in Indian Culture works in circles—and that everything is connected and that coming to terms with one's mental health is a personal journey that involves individuals, families and communities" (quoted in NAMI 2003).

Suicide is one topic addressed in a 2012 report by the Northwest Portland Area Indian Health Board on recent mortality patterns. The report examines the leading causes of death in 2006–2009 in the Northwest states of Idaho, Washington, and Oregon and compares data for the AI/AN community with that for the white population in an effort to address racial disparities while informing public health decision-making. The report found that suicide rates for the AI/AN population was the seventh leading cause of death, with a rate of 3.1 percent, as compared to a rate of 1.9 percent for the white population. Suicides accounted for approximately one fifth of all AI/AN injury deaths in the region for the time period (Northwest Portland Area Indian Health Board 2012, 10).

A reporter for the *Billings Gazette* asserts that the factors putting Indian children at risk for suicide are amplified for those living on Indian reservations (Thackeray 2011). Thackeray states that "Indian children are more likely to be abused, see their mothers being abused, and live in a household where someone is controlled by drugs and alcohol. They have the highest rates of emotional and physical neglect, and are more likely to be exposed to trauma." As cited by Thackeray, Delores Subia Big Foot, PhD (Caddo Nation of Oklahoma), testified to the United States Senate Committee on Indian Affairs, stating that "American Indian / Alaska Native children and youth experience an increased risk of multiple victimizations" (Subia Big Foot 2009, 22) and feel a lack of safety in their environments. Their environments include a high rate of poverty which is generational and community deep (Subia Big Foot 2009; Thackeray 2011). Poverty and unemployment rates are high on Montana Indian reservations. In 2015 the *Great Falls Tribune* reported that my reservation, Rocky Boy, had an unemployment rate of 9.6 percent, according to the Montana Department of Labor and Industry (Baumann 2015). I doubt that the unemployment rate is that low. The tribe itself in *Native News Project* 2012 projected the unemployment rate to be 70 percent in the summer months, with it rising to 80 percent during the winter (Lungren 2012).

Suicide is an immense problem for the tribes of Montana, including the Chippewa Cree. In an attempt to locate suicide statistics, I spoke with the tribal Behavioral Health Department, which is part of the Rocky Boy Health Board. They do not keep statistics regarding suicide and referred me to the Billings office of Indian Health Services (IHS), who referred me to their website, where I gathered the following information: "Suicide data is crucial in understanding and preventing suicides on the Reservations in Montana and Wyoming. However, suicide data on Montana Reservations are severely underreported. There are only a few agencies in the community that collect suicide data, which is generally not shared between agencies offering treatment or other services to suicidal individuals and/or their family members" (Rocky Mountain Tribal Epidemiology Center 2010, 15). There is a grant initiative, the Suicide Data Tracking Project, designed to augment the current IHS suicide tracking database. The plan is for the data to be used to understand suicide and suicide attempts on the reservation and to plan interventions (Rocky Mountain Tribal Epidemiology Center 2010).

The tribes of Montana are acutely aware that suicide has reached an epidemic crisis for their people. Cindy Uken reported in the *Missoulian* on the solutions that Montana tribes were seeking in the effort to reduce suicides (Uken 2013). When Uken asked who is at the greatest risk, the Fort Peck Indian Tribe's suicide prevention coordinator responded, "Everybody. I don't have a specific gender. I don't have a specific age group." Once again, the lack of safe communities, safe schools, and safe families were cited as an indicator and cause of the suicide epidemic.

The article brought to light a critical facet of Native American culture offered by Gordon Belcourt (Blackfeet), then executive director of the Montana-Wyoming Tribal Leaders Council. Belcourt shared with Uken that it is only in the last twenty to thirty years that Native Americans have begun to talk about suicide. To speak of it is still considered culturally taboo in many tribes. There is a common saying among Native people that we carry our problems silently.

As a Cree person, I was taught that people who kill themselves must wander the Earth alone until the time the Creator intended for the end of their lives. If someone is fortunate, intervention from the other side may occur. One of my nephews attempted to kill himself. He was between this world and the next. He heard the voices of his uncles who had walked on; they told him, "Go back, go back, it isn't your time yet." He was able to have victory over the spirit of suicide that had overtaken him, and he came back to the living.

There is much work being done in Indian Country to support the healing of women, including Native American women experiencing incarceration. It would be inappropriate for me to share confidential practices from my tribe as well as from tribes in which I am not a member. Fortunately, I am able to share healing practices where the information has been published, therefore making it public, and where appropriate, Cree healing modalities will be shared.

In their book *Native American Postcolonial Psychology*, Eduardo Duran (Navajo-Apache) and Bonnie Duran (Opelousas-Coushatta) assert that the pain suffered by many Native individuals and communities is a direct result of colonization. They advocate for a postcolonial paradigm where knowledge is accepted from different cosmologies, and where they are validated and legitimized without having to adhere to the larger dominant culture. They contend that communities' Indigenous forms of knowledge have always been and will always be relevant in the overcoming and the healing process for Native people with respect to the Native cosmology (Duran and Duran 1995).

Duran and Duran (1995) respectfully acknowledge that it is difficult to describe the Native American worldview aptly in a succinct yet encompassing manner, given that whole books have been written on the subject. They stress that the Native American worldview is not, as discussed, one of compartmentalization, where the mind and body are separated from the mind and spirit. Additionally, Native American people do not see themselves as separate from creation but rather are part of this world and the next and all that is animate and inanimate. "The need for healing can be explained by the fact that the client/community has lost the ability to be in harmony with the life process of which the client/community is a part" (Duran and Duran 1995, 15). In order to understand and validate the healing ceremonies of Native American people, those from outside the culture need to suspend judgment and respect the cosmology of Native people.

The worldview of Natives is the cultural lens through which we view the world and make sense of it. Iris Heavy Runner (Blackfeet) and Joann

Sebastian Morris (Sault Ste. Marie Chippewa) list ten commonalities that can be found among the federally recognized tribes. There were 554 such tribes in 1997 when their work was published; there are currently 567 and the First Nations of Canada. These core values, beliefs, and behaviors are integral to our worldview. They are

spirituality
child-rearing / extended family
veneration of age/wisdom/tradition
respect for nature
generosity and sharing
cooperation / group harmony
autonomy / respect for others
composure/patience
relativity of time
nonverbal communication (Heavy Runner and Morris 1997, 1)

Heavy Runner and Morris (1997) provide insight to the importance of spirituality to Native people:

Spirituality is a fundamental, continuous part of our lives. In traditional times, spirituality was integral to one's daily life. Embodied in Native spirituality is the concept of interconnectedness. The spiritual nature of all living things was recognized and respected. The mystical aspects of life were openly discussed. A strong ceremonial practice was interwoven into the cycle of seasons. Ceremonies marked important times in people's lives, such as children's naming ceremonies or puberty rites. Spirituality is at the core of our survival. Many Native educators agree that our spirituality has been the cornerstone of our survival through generations of adversity and oppression. Traditional people approach Indian spirituality with tremendous care and respect. (1–2)

As stated earlier, I am able to share cultural and spiritual information that is either publicly available or for which I am given permission to do so by an Elder. I am practicing the utmost care in deciding what to share, as it must come from within my culture. There are many charlatans and people who choose to co-opt Native American cultural and spiritual practices. Sadly, these charlatans are not only from outside our culture but also from inside our culture. I am holding this process before Creator and the Ancestors as I have been taught that if my intentions and actions are in a good way then I can leave Creator to deal with the imposters.

THE MEDICINE WHEEL

FourDirectionsTeachings.com is a project created to share Indigenous knowledge and philosophy for educators to incorporate into their curriculum. The National Advisory Committee approached the Elders and traditional teachers. On the site, Cree Elder Mary Lee shares teachings about Cree beliefs (Lee 2006). She begins by sharing the following:

> As Cree people, we were given the gift of being named for the four parts of human beings. *Nehiyawak*, we were called.
>
> It means being balanced in the four parts that are found in the four directions of the Medicine Wheel. These four parts for human beings are the spiritual, physical, emotional, and mental aspects of the self. We need to try and balance these four parts that were given to us, to function as people.
>
> The fire is in the centre of the Medicine Wheel. That is where the meaning of the teachings comes from. For me this fire is also the self. When you look at the Medicine Wheel, you start from self. And as you look out, you make your circle.
>
> This is how the Medicine Wheel represents the life journey of people.
>
> The old people will tell you it is life itself. Look at the four seasons and follow the sun. Spring in the east, summer in the south, fall in the west and winter in the north. It tells the whole story of how all life came into being abundantly bright, rising in the east and then fading away as it moves west and north. All life rises and sets like the sun.
>
> What we do in between is our journey. This is where the gifts of the four directions are needed—the gifts of the spirit, physical body, emotions and mind—and where we need to find balance within these four realms. Today, many people are out of balance because they tend to only favour two realms of self, the mental and the physical. They forget to look after

their spiritual side, and often don't know how to express and deal with their emotions. . . .

As for the spirit, there never seems to be enough time. People think you have to make a commitment of time through long periods of devotion to be spiritual. But being spiritual is remembering. It is remembering that the first thing that was gifted to you when you came into being was the spirit. Sadly, we tend to forget that and then we neglect our spirit and take it for granted. So we need to remember where we came from and the gifts that were given to us as human beings.

This way of being in the world was taught to me by my mother through the teachings of making a tipi. The tipi teachings, as I call them today, relate to nurturing the four aspects of the self, the spiritual, physical, emotional and mental, which are rooted in the four directions.

There are women older than me who are sometimes made to feel that, because they don't have the English language or education, they don't have a right to speak. But those are the powerful ones, the sacred ones, because they were not disrupted in their journey. My mother was one of those women. Her knowledge was pure, uninterrupted by residential school. It wasn't written knowledge; it was a life she lived.

My mother spoke only Cree. From a very early age, she instilled in her children the value of our culture and language. She had two daughters and five sons. All of us speak Cree and have gone to ceremonies like the Sun Dance and the Sweat Lodge since we were little children. She shared with us the teachings and meanings of these ceremonies. And she also shared her teachings with women in the community, because she was given the gift of helping women in their journey to becoming mothers. In English, a rough analogy is in the word *midwife*. Many of her teachings to me were about the sacredness of motherhood and how to help women raise healthy children in the world. She retained these teachings because her life was not interrupted by residential school. So, she was able to parent differently, with the knowledge that was given to her as a child. That is why I say all of my teachings—everything I know—came from her.

Everything my mother learned came from her grandmother, who raised her when both of her parents died. So, she learned everything from two generations before her. I am fortunate; because of my great-grandmother and mother, I can share the teachings that at one time were known to all Cree women, like the teepee teachings and teachings on the value of women. So, in honor of Cree women everywhere I will share these teachings with you. (Lee 2006)

It is important to note that the Medicine Wheel is interpreted differently for different tribes. In fact, the design of the wheel varies from tribe to tribe. Unlike Western spirituality, where some religions view their relation as the "one true way," tribes do not consider their model and interpretation as "right" and that of other tribes "wrong." There are, however, some commonalities:

It is a circle because life is occurring in a circle because all things return to where they began.
The center has meaning and is central to the teachings.
It is sacred.
The sections, often called spokes, represent the cycle of life tied with nature.
No section is more important than the other, rather the philological and psychological journey of where we began life as a child to where we progress to being an Elder is represented in all the stages, just like all the seasons of nature are cyclical.

The Cree Medicine Wheel and its four directions—physical, spiritual, emotional, and mental—provides a guide for Cree people to find balance and healing (Lee 2006). It also portrays the journey of life from childhood to gaining eldership. It is an instrument of sacred cultural learning for the body, mind, and spirit.

The Medicine Wheel is an important tool of healing. Annie Wenger-Nabigon (Oji-Cree) describes the sacredness of the Medicine Wheel and stresses that "it is a pathway for healing among many aboriginal peoples across the continent, used in reclaiming identity and purpose for individuals and communities" (Wenger-Nabigon 2010, 142). She uses the Medicine Wheel in her work with strengthening relationships within Indigenous peoples, communities, and families. She conveys her understanding of Medicine Wheel teachings as a conduit to "learning the techniques, methods, and practices, involved in making decisions, taking risk, maintaining relationships, handling emotions, learning difficult tasks, practicing caring behaviors and taking responsibility for oneself" (Wenger-Nabigon 2010, 156).

The teachings and ceremonies of the Medicine Wheel are about balance, interconnectedness with all of creation, and relationships. They are about the knowledge and spirituality that Creator and the Ancestors provide in this world and the next. Learning and applying the knowledge of the Medicine Wheel is an act of healing.

SWEAT LODGE

Tribal cultures vary in the design and building of sweat lodges. The knowledge of how to build a sweat lodge is passed down from generation to generation. The ceremonies, songs, and protocols of building and using the sweat lodge are particular to the tribe. According to Anishnawbe Mushkiki (2022), "The Sweat Lodge has been called 'the most powerful structure in the world.' Sweats vary from purification and cleansing to healing sweats. It is said that the Sweat lodge ceremony 'responds' to what the people need. Other types of sweats include clan sweats, such as Bear clan sweats, sweats for fasters, sundancers and sweats when you seek your spirit name."

The Ancestors visioned the sweat lodge as a gift from the Creator to help in healing, purification, and connection to the spirit world.

> The Sweatlodge ceremony is a sacred purification ceremony conducted by a trained lodge keeper. The Cree and Ojibway learned the sweatlodge from the Arapaho, Sioux and Blackfeet and combined them into their own culture. There are several kinds of sweatlodge ceremonies that a lodge keeper may conduct such as, teaching, healing, community, children's, Bear, Buffalo, Eagle, Turtle, eight-star teaching, contrary and solstice/ equinox sweatlodge ceremonies.
>
> To enter the sweatlodge is to return to the womb of Mother Earth for purification, strength, guidance, and physical, mental, emotional, and spiritual healing. Grandfather rocks, wood, fire, and water are used in the process. Participants in a healing lodge offer their prayers for individuals

who are unwell spiritually emotionally physically and mentally. Prayers are offered to family members, friends or work groups who are unable to attend the lodge. Everything about the sweatlodge is ceremonial and sacred, from the construction of the sweatlodge, altar, fire pit, to the use of fire, care, and cleansing of sweatlodge grounds.

To begin the sweatlodge ceremony the fire keepers set up the fire pit with wood and rocks (grandfathers) creating a wood structure bed for the grandfathers to sit on. Tobacco and prayers are offered to the first four cardinal directions grandfathers placed giving thanks to them for giving of their spirit to assist in the healing of the people. A wood structure that is built in the middle of the fire pit. It is lit with wooden matches using strips of kindling collected from the birch bark tree family. The rocks are warmed by fire element for up to 1½ to 2 hours until the rocks are amber orange. In the warming up process with the sacred fire the medicine from the tree family is absorbed and blessed into the rocks. When the grandfathers are ready the fire keeper will notify the sweatlodge conductor that the womb of Mother Earth is ready to be entered.

All in attendance are given a teaching about the sacred fire and sweatlodge teachings before entering. The area between the fire and center of the sweatlodge is sacred. It is the cedar trail that represents the umbilical cord from the sacred fire to the inside center of the lodge. This cedar trail is not to be walked over. Attendees are provided with a smudge of cedar medicine and are given tobacco to offer to the sacred fire their prayer requests before entering the sweatlodge. Nothing other than tobacco when entering the lodge is to be placed into the Sacred Fire unless requested by the Sweatlodge conductor throughout the beginning and end of ceremony. The Sacred Fire is tended by the fire keeper or a designated helper for safety reasons and fire keeper responsibilities.

The Sweatlodge conductor enters first, the individuals asked to sit in cardinal directions, east, south, west, and north [enter] next followed by attendees. When everyone has entered the sweatlodge and are sitting the fire keepers brings in the first-round community of grandfather rocks. The sacred pipe(s) are lifted, and a pipe ceremony is conducted together with a traditional pipe song sung to honour the pipe(s) smoked to initiate the ceremony. The pipe carrier(s) follows their pipe ceremony protocol, requesting prayers and healing with each seven cardinal directions.

After the pipe is smoked the fire keepers are requested to close the door to begin the first round/doorway of the east direction. Cedar medicine is poured on the grandfathers and grandmother. The sacred eagle whistle is sounded to request the presence of the spirit animals and ancestors to assist in healing. Sacred prayer songs are sung to honour the spirit helpers according to the type of sweatlodge being conducted. There are four levels of prayers and many sacred songs sung called "rounds" or "doorways." Each round/doorway ends with a prayer or shout as the door flap is thrown open and the cool breath of the Creator welcomes all into new life.

Even though the fire keeper is not inside the sweatlodge, he/she is very much a part of the ceremony and may receive teachings, cleansing, and healing. In some teachings, the rocks are known as the bones of Mother Earth. The fire keeper responsibility is to oversee the outside circle of the lodge including the sacred fire, cedar medicine, door openings between rounds, grandfathers in the fire pit bed, wood usage, tobacco offerings, and most importantly the spiritual care and safety of the attendees inside the sweatlodge.

The lodge itself is usually a dome-shaped structure of willow or other saplings indigenous to the area, tied together with cloth. The structure is then covered with a tarpaulin, blankets, or canvas to make it light proof. As a vessel for the grandfathers, a small pit is dug in the center of the lodge. The doorway may face east or west according to indigenous practices of the lodge keeper/conductor.

Outside the lodge, a small earthen mound is built as a sacred altar, using tree stumps or dirt from the pit inside. Beyond the altar is the fire pit for heating the rocks. A pitchfork and/or shovel are needed to carry the grandfather rocks into the lodge. The grandfather rocks are laid onto a plywood board. Grandfather rocks are brought in at the beginning of the rounds or doors on the plywood board, deer antlers are used to maneuver the grandfather rocks inside the sweatlodge circle bed. Cedar medicine is sprinkled on the hot rocks, producing steam mist and heat. (Gikinoo'amaage, n.d.)

The sweat lodge provides healing, purification, connection to Creator, Nature, and each other while creating balance in one's life. The sweat lodge is a gift from Creator, and the knowledge to practice its medicine comes through the Ancestors. The helping spirits give guidance.

SMUDGING

Native people use smudging as a purification ceremony. The protocols may vary slightly from tribe to tribe, but the core concepts are the same. A group of stakeholders and Elders developed the following guidelines for smudging in Manitoba schools, where First Nations, including Cree, Inuit, and Métis, are highly represented in the student body:

> Many First Nations share the concept of "mino-pimatisiwin," which means "good life" in both Cree and Ojibwe. Implicit in this is the understanding that all of life is a ceremony; that the sacred and the secular are parts of the whole; that people are whole beings (body, mind, spirit, emotion); and that "mino-pimatisiwin" is achieved by taking care of all aspects of one's self.
>
> Smudging is a tradition, common to many First Nations, which involves the burning of one or more medicines gathered from the earth. The four sacred medicines used in First Nations' ceremonies are tobacco, sage, cedar and sweetgrass. The most common medicines used in a smudge are sweetgrass, sage and cedar.
>
> Smudging has been passed down from generation to generation. There are many ways and variations on how a smudge is done. Historically, Métis and Inuit people did not smudge; however, today many Métis and Inuit people have incorporated smudging into their lives.
>
> A community Grandmother presented the following as the steps and rationale for this cleansing process we call smudge to Niji Mahkwa School in Winnipeg:
>
> We smudge to clear the air around us.
>
> We smudge to clean our minds so that we will have good thoughts of others.
>
> We smudge our eyes so that we will only see the good in others.
>
> We smudge our ears so that we will only listen to positive things about others.
>
> We smudge our mouths so that we will only speak well of others.

We smudge our whole being so we will portray only the good part of our self through our actions.

Smudging allows people to stop, slow down, become mindful and centred. This allows people to remember, connect and be grounded in the event, task or purpose at hand. Smudging also allows people to let go of something negative. Letting go of things that inhibit a person from being balanced and focused comes from the feeling of being calm and safe while smudging. The forms of smudging will vary from nation to nation but are considered by all to be a way of cleansing oneself. Smudging is part of "the way things are done" and is part of living a good life.

Smudging is always voluntary. People should never be forced or pressured to smudge. It is completely acceptable for a person to indicate that he/she does not want to smudge and that person may choose to stay in the room and refrain or leave the room during a smudge. Respect for all is the guiding principle in any Aboriginal tradition.

The act of clearing the air, mind, spirit and emotions may be accomplished in a variety of ways but according to First Nations' practice, a smudge is led by a person who has an understanding of what a smudge is and why it is done. That person may be an Elder or cultural teacher who has been invited into the school; it can be a staff person who is knowledgeable about the tradition of smudging; it can be a parent/guardian; and/or it can be a student.

The medicine is placed in a smudge container. The container may be a shell, a ceramic or stone bowl, a copper, brass or cast iron pan. The medicine is lit with a match. Once the medicine is lit, the smoke may be pushed forward with a feather or a fan. The person who lights the smudge is first.

The commonly used medicine is sage. A "smudge ball" is created mainly from the leaf of the plant, which is rolled into a ball for burning. It is important to understand that this particular medicine can create a significant billow of smoke, which emerges from the smudge ball. It is not necessary to create enough smoke to fill the entire space where a group is smudging. Only a small stream of smoke for the person who is smudging is required. Therefore, it is important for the helpers who create the smudge ball to keep it relatively small.

When we smudge, we first cleanse our hands with the smoke as if we were washing our hands. We then draw the smoke over our heads, eyes, ears, mouths and our bodies. These actions remind us to think good thoughts, see good actions, hear good sounds, speak good words and show the good of who we are. (Aboriginal Education Directorate 2014, 3–5)

Smudging is an integral part of Native spirituality and is done both on a regular basis and for specific purposes, such as when one prepares to speak, sing, play the drum, attend a ceremony, or participate in a Talking Circle. We strive to find the good part of ourselves and others. We seek balance within ourselves and connection to each other and Creator.

THE NEED FOR HEALING CEREMONIES

In discussing the need for healing ceremonies there is a direct correlation between the experience of colonization of First Nations people of Canada and Native American tribes. Lee Maracle (Canadian First Nations Coast Salish) expresses a truth that, while painful to hear and accept, is nevertheless essential as part of the healing process for Indigenous people of this continent. Lateral oppression and hatred are two corollary aspects of historical trauma. She describes it as the result of accumulated anger from generation to generation, where members of the victimized race work out anticolonial rage against our own people, hating ourselves and each other (Maracle 1996). Maracle asserts that this self-hate is not real, rather it is a cover for the systemic rage within our people. She acknowledges her own sickened spirit needed to be healed and to find that healing she sought the teachings of her grandmothers.

Maracle (1996) discusses the distortion of traditionalism, which has occurred in a number of ways, including the portrayal of Indigenous people of this continent as savage, primitive, and unintelligent. In contrast, we have also been presented in a romanticized manner, which fails to recognize the layers of our lives from family, tribal, government, intertribal interactions, cultural norms, differences, and way of life determined by environment and spirituality. She stresses that our people have always had their cultural origins and that culture is a living thing. She eloquently states, "The philosophical premise of a people rarely alters itself fundamentally" (110). Maracle describes culture as a mirror of a people's way of life. The search for truth and healing is answered in the ceremonies of our grandmothers. She reminds us that "spirituality is re-connecting with the self and our ancestry. It is doing the right thing for your family and your community" (134).

HEALING CEREMONIES—CHIPPEWA CREE OF ROCKY BOY'S

On a visit home I had the honor of spending time with some of my Elders. While I cannot share all of the information that they shared with me, I do have their permission to share some of the knowledge passed on to me. First of all, in the Cree culture, I can only ask questions about ceremony with a woman Elder. It is inappropriate to discuss ways of women with men. Secondly, they must be approached in a good way. This means that someone from my family, in my case my sister-in-law and my nieces, interceded on my behalf, asking if they would be so kind as to spend some time with me and answer some questions for me. Thirdly, I must bring a gift. The gift can be sage or sweetgrass, or fabric, and must include tobacco.

Spending time with my Elders was a magnificent experience. The first part of the process was for me to introduce myself and tell them who my people are so that they can place me and my ancestors. Those who knew my grandparents and mother well spoke a few words about them. They had many questions about my life from the time I was taken away up until now. A couple of them remembered me as a young child and commented on the difficult childhood and living circumstances of my family and our family troubles.

My Elders shared with me that traditionally Cree women did not participate in the sweat lodge and that it is only in contemporary times that it has become a part of women's healing. Some of them participate in the sweat lodge and some do not. When I discussed the grief and shame that I have encountered working with Native American women experiencing incarceration they shared that there is a grief ceremony that Cree women can go through. All that a woman needs to do is to approach one of her Elders and speak of her need. They felt that the women in prison would greatly benefit from the ceremony, which can be called a "Wiping of Tears" ceremony, as part of their healing practices. Most importantly they encouraged daily prayer to Creator, smudging, and spending time with Elders.

The need for healing and processing grief was discussed in my Native circle of association in Portland. A young woman in the group, Andrea Robideau (paternal affiliations Spirit Lake Nation–Sisseton/Wahpeton Bands of Dakota and White Earth Nation–Anishinaabe; maternal affiliations Mescalero Apache, Yaqui, Tsalagi, Cherokee from Oklahoma), whose mother was a highly respected Elder who passed away in 2016, humbly shared these wise words with us:

> Prepare a traditional meal—gather relatives and tribal members together—invite tribal leaders and elders in the ways you were taught (give them a gift with a personal invite—let them know why you need their participation)—invite the people (Creator will make it possible for the people who need to be there to be present, whether it is a very small group at a kitchen table or a large community gathering at a traditional gathering place).
>
> Proceed in a ceremonial way (blessing songs/prayers to invite ancestors in the way your tribe/people practice [i.e., for some tribes it is smudging or blessing water])—proceed with facilitating & speaking from your heart with your request to learn and understand more about traditional ways of grieving that you / the community can then revitalize—open the floor up for the eldest folks to share and then go around the group (like a talking circle) to hear and learn from folks about what bits and pieces they were taught or what they remember (and maybe why those practices we stopped or put aside) . . . at the end, share the meal together—their spirits and their bodies will have been fed . . . seeds of positive change or healthy ways of grieving will have been planted. You are already planting seeds by simply asking the questions.
>
> If you go forward to share what you have learned, it is okay for folks to hire you/*anyone else in particular* as a facilitator to share about experiences and teachings that you/they have been given permission to share—they are not hiring you / that person to pray, even if you/they

do decide to pray with/for the group—it's important to clarify that they are hiring a facilitator to begin a task of gathering people in a good way and following through with all necessary facilitating/coordinating tasks.

*Our elders often have more practice and wisdom at this sort of thing because they've witnessed so much in their lifetimes and have more experience. However, young folks carry tremendous healing energy as well and can be very effective as facilitators. Have you ever witnessed the effects of little children visiting elder homes? The energy of children is rejuvenating—strive to create/facilitate intergenerational gatherings.

Set out offerings (whatever you were taught: food, medicine plants, etc.) to thank the spirits of ancestors that were present during the gathering. Religious and spiritual groups all have some form of offering/giving in that way—do what you were taught with an open heart (in a good way).

Always follow up with getting feedback from participants: in closing, during clean up, in the days after, in the weeks/months after, and a year later . . . because THAT is how we nurture the seeds—that is how we maintain the relationships and bonds developed/strengthened through these facilitated practices . . . and relationships are why these teachings were requested in the first place.

Creator put something special in each and every one of us . . . part of that "something special" are intuitive instructions of how to take care of each other in a good way. Sometimes we just need help remembering.

Thank you for helping me remember this much for today. You've inspired me to share this for my loved-ones and relatives. Wherever we are: we are family and we help one-another grow.

I ask humble forgiveness and patience if I have offended anyone with these words—and I welcome feedback or corrections that will help correct my steps along the path that I walk. (A. Robideau, personal communication, November 30, 2016)

As my trip home came to a close, one of my Elders who knew my mother and our family story took my hands in hers and looked deeply into my eyes and told me, "You're alright. Your eyes are clear." I cannot begin to express how deeply her words and her medicine touched my soul.

The need for healing cannot be more highly stressed, not only for the Native American women experiencing incarceration but for all Native people. The traumas of our ancestors run through the generations of our families, and if they remain unaddressed, the societal ills of our people will only increase. There is hope and that hope lies in access to ceremony and Elders. Providing access to culture and traditional ways is best done from within a community by Elders and spiritual leaders. However, the method by which that knowledge is imparted is essential to it being received, understood, and practiced by those in need of that knowledge. Each tribal community has their own ways of teaching and passing on information and practices.

Traditional ways unfortunately have been affected by the larger dominant society and colonization. My best example is this: if we were indeed passing on traditional knowledge and ways of being in the world in a "good way," we would not have the societal ills that we have today, including the over-incarceration of our people. In examining the issue of the incarceration of Native women and considering my role, and my own way of being in the world, I was drawn to gentle action theory.

CHAPTER 5

Gentle Action Theory

F. DAVID PEAT, PHD

I was first introduced to both Dr. Peat and gentle action theory as a PhD student where the theory was part of our coursework. Dr. Peat was a professor, a theoretical physicist, and an author. As part of my coursework I began contemplating gentle action theory in my research into Native American women's experiences of incarceration. Dr. Peat and I had some discussions on traditional ways and the juxtaposition of gentle action theory. Dr. Peat was

> a quantum physicist, writer, and teacher who founded The Pari Center in 2000. He wrote more than 20 books which have been translated into 24 languages, as well as numerous essays and articles. In 1971–72, he spent a sabbatical year with Roger Penrose and David Bohm, and thereafter his research focused on the foundations of quantum theory and on a non-unitary approach to the quantum measurement problem. Peat continued an active collaboration with Bohm and in 1987 they co-authored the book *Science, Order and Creativity*. David Peat died, in Pari, in 2017. (Pari Center, n.d.)

Dr. Peat, in his book *Blackfoot Physics: A Journey into the Native American Worldview*, shared his experience about when he went to the Blackfoot Sun Dance ceremony in Alberta, Canada.

Hitherto having spent all his life steeped in and influenced by linear Western science, he was entranced by the Native world view and, through dialogue circles between scientists and Native Elders, he began to explore it in greater depth. *Blackfoot Physics* is the account of his discoveries. In an edifying synthesis of anthropology, history, metaphysics, cosmology and quantum theory, Peat compares the medicines, the myths, the languages, indeed the entire perceptions of reality of two peoples: Western and Indigenous. What becomes apparent is the amazing resemblance between Indigenous teachings and some of the insights that are emerging from modern science, a congruence that is as enlightening about the physical universe as it is about the circular evolution of man's understanding. (Peat 2022)

Dr. Peat shares his perspective in discussing his book *Blackfoot Physics: A Journey into the Native American Worldview*:

A DIALOGUE BETWEEN WORLDS

It is in such a spirit, and with such an aim, that this book is written. This is not a book "about" Native American society, or "about" Indigenous knowledge. It is certainly not the result of objective academic study. Rather it is an exploration of two different ways of knowing, two different worlds of consciousness and a discovery of the ways that peoples can begin to dialogue with each other, enter into relationship, and offer each other the respect and courtesy that is the hallmark of humanity. (Peat 2022, ch. 1)

Getting to know Dr. Peat and reading both *Blackfoot Physics: A Journey into the Native American Worldview* (2005) and *Gentle Action: Bringing Creative Change to a Turbulent World* (2008), I knew that I wanted to work with him on my research and writing.

DEFINITION

Gentle action is an approach that begins from within a system where new forms of gentle action are developed to address societal issues in creative ways prior to taking action (Peat 2008). F. David Peat explains that gentle action theory is an alternative to previously employed methods historically applied in both research and application in Indian Country, as further elaborated on later. It is an approach that begins with an initial "creative suspension" of action. Gentle action is unlike the typical Western idea that one must do something and that it must be done right now. Instead, gentle action allows for dialogue and time for creativity in pondering solutions and designing activities. By contrast to Western ways of responding, traditional ways of knowing and being seek harmony in all living things, and time and space are created for the process, versus rushing in with the potential to do more harm than good. Gentle action theory connects well with Chippewa Cree collectivist culture and values of interconnectedness.

GENTLE ACTION

F. David Peat (2008) termed his theory of gentle action upon his belief that solutions to societal issues, when done in a gentle way, result in forming different kinds of actions. These actions come from within systems as opposed to outside forces. He calls for a process that begins with "creative suspension," where we pause, listen, and learn about the system. Only when we are open to holding space can we learn what the system should teach us before acting. Peat began using the term "gentle action" several years ago, when describing activities and actions while being sensitive to environmental dynamics of people within the system and those interacting with the system of people and the issues at play.

Important facets of his theory include its subtlety, a call for minimal intervention, and sensitivity in guidance. Instead of seeking control, gentle action seeks harmony by listening and learning about the people, society, and issues as opposed to exerting power and control over a situation. Gentle action seeks to guide and act in a sensitive manner.

A core objective of gentle action is to develop a perception that is as clear as possible about a given situation for those involved and those called upon to assist, be it directly or indirectly. It is imperative to acknowledge that we all bring our own perceptions and prejudices to every situation we encounter, which are based on our own experiences and belief systems. The more aware we are of our own context, the more we are present and able to process information about the situation and the community needs. A basis of action can be generated that is flexible, sensitive, and creative, resulting in appropriate and harmonious action (Peat 2008). Trust is essential in employing gentle action, as all people involved must be trustworthy and truthful for the community members to bring their best abilities to the project. Creative action built on trust can change the social fabric of a community in need (Peat 2008).

Gentle action refocuses the energies and dynamics of the group to co-create solutions as a new "social organism." In describing gentle action theory, Peat (2008) offers a metaphor: what if all the wavelets around the edges of a pond could cooperatively coalesce toward a predetermined area? What would result would be an action internal to the system versus an external action, such as what happens when a pebble is thrown into the pond, creating a movement of the whole body of water. Similarly, when a system or group performs in a coordinated, way a significant change can occur in addressing a societal issue.

The Gentle Action website provides cases where the theory has been used; one case highlighted is a literacy project in India (Gentle Action, n.d.). According to Peat, the first Indo-International School in Dundlod, a remote village in India, was started in 1996 by the participants of the State University of New York (SUNY) Oneonta "Learn and Serve" study abroad program. The Ninash's Star school began with fifty underprivileged (Dalit) children and grew to five hundred students from nursery to high school. The school is a miracle of triumph in the middle of the desert. The school for lower-caste children came about through the efforts of three individuals in the SUNY Oneonta program. Philosophy professor Ashok Malhotra was leading a semester in India program, and while preparing the students for their experience, shared with them the living conditions of the children in the village. The people in the village were living in extreme poverty. A student in the program, Josie Basile, felt compelled to act to address the situation and serve the children and families. She raised almost $5,000 to help launch the school. Suzanne Miller, an education professor, provided her expertise as an educator and drew on her experience as a former Peace Corps volunteer to create the educational program. Working with the women in the village, they obtained a donation of a one-room building (F. D. Peat, personal communication, 2016).

By 2007 a road was built to connect the main road to the school. Funding for the road came from the Ninash Foundation, through donations from the Oneonta community, resulting in 30 percent of the funds. The remaining 70 percent of funding came from the village of Dundlod. Dr. Malhotra founded the Ninash Foundation in memory of his wife to "promote literacy among children and adults throughout the world" and the foundation has established an endowment for the school to ensure that funds will always be available to pay teachers (SUNY Oneonta, n.d.). A celebration was held in 2007 where thirty-five milk-producing goats were given to the people in the greatest need in Dundlod. The Oneonta community and students from Greater Plains Elementary raised funds to purchase the goats. In addition, the children of the Riverside School raised $450 and purchased seven hundred books that were donated to the Dundlod school library as part of the Oneonta Sister City project.

The highlight of the celebration was that two students from Dundlod school had been admitted to college. Prior to the school, the children's only future was selling dung. Breaking through the barriers of class, religion, and gender provides a model and inspiration for students at the school and the community. The project, which began in the hearts of three people and grew to include hundreds, is an impressive example of gentle action theory.

A second case from the Gentle Action website is from Marilyn Fowler. Marilyn lived in northern California, where San Ramon Creek ran behind her home. She was concerned about the San Ramon Creek watershed, which is one of the five main sub-watersheds of the Walnut Creek Watershed, with the San Ramon Creek watershed covering approximately fifty-four square miles. Marilyn had become very frustrated trying to work her way through the various bureaucracies that manage the creek. She read the book *Gentle Action: Bringing Creative Change to a Turbulent World* (Peat 2008) and was struck by Peat's example of Gordon Shippey's story.

Gordon and his wife Claire lived in Middlesbrough, an industrial village in northeast England. The Shippeys' neighborhood was marred with garbage, abandoned cars, crime, unemployment, and drugs, with no safe places for children to play and showing a breakdown of community relationships. After a visit to Paris and Italy, and spending time with

F. David Peat, the Shippeys decided to put gentle action in to practice upon returning home.

Gordon, realizing that they did not even know their neighbors, decided to knock on each neighbor's door, introducing himself. He got to know two of his neighbors well, and they along with Claire formed a group to address the issues in their neighborhood. They created a video and photo account of some of the problems in the neighborhood, which they presented to their local council, who took some measures to tackle some of the problems. After the founding of the neighborhood group, Gordon noticed neighbors beginning to talk with each other and children beginning to play outside. The group continued to work together on issues in the neighborhood. They have built community. They have collaborated with local businesses, the university, the government, and the police.

Inspired by the Shippeys, Marilyn Fowler realized that she too needed her neighbors. She walked down her street, knocking on doors, introducing herself to her neighbors. She feels that it made all the difference. She now has others who share her concerns about the creek. They went on to form the Friends of the San Ramon Creek alliance. She is grateful for the model of gentle action. Gentle action theory revealed to Fowler that she needed her neighbors. She needed them on several levels. She needed those who shared common concerns about San Ramon Creek, she needed the sense of community, and while she could have championed the cause on her own, she needed the social power that occurs when people band together for a shared cause. The model of gentle action moved Fowler and her community to actions that were sensitive, flexible, and creative.

RELEVANCE OF GENTLE ACTION THEORY FOR INDIAN COUNTRY

The theory can find practical application in conjunction with traditional ways of knowing and being in Indian Country and, in particular, working with Native American women experiencing incarceration. Gentle action (Peat 2008) emphasizes a kinder, gentler, creative, and flexible process. A fundamental element of the theory is that the process begins inside a system.

For too long Native Americans have had outsiders come into our communities telling us what our problems are and how to fix them, using an arrogant power to insert themselves. One notorious such example is the Diabetes Project with the Havasupai Tribe, conducted by researchers from Arizona State University (Mello and Wolf 2010).

In 1989 Rex Tilousi, a tribal member, met with an Arizona State University (ASU) anthropologist, John Martin, and asked for a referral to a doctor who specialized in type 2 diabetes care to work with the tribe and stop the spread of the disease. Martin contacted Dr. Markow, a human genetics professor, to support the tribe. The university funded Dr. Markow's work to study type 2 diabetes in the tribe. However, according to the *New York Times*, Dr. Markow's research interests also included schizophrenia, and researchers gathered blood and obtained broad consent forms indicating that the research was to "study the causes of behavioral/medical disorders" (Harmon 2010). This study was done without Martin's knowledge or that of the Havasupai people.

The consent form is described as "purposely simple" because English was a second language for many Havasupai people. During his work with the tribe, Markow marked several genes searching for multiple disorders, including schizophrenia and alcoholism. The tribal research participants did not know that the research would be used for those purposes and felt shame when articles were published.

The Havasupai people live in a remote part of the Grand Canyon and have had a high rate of type 2 diabetes. The researchers began a research project which included health education, the collecting and testing of blood samples, as well as genetic testing in an effort to find links between genes and diabetes risk. The Arizona State researchers were not successful in finding a genetic link to type 2 diabetes, but unbeknownst to the Havasupai people, the ASU researchers then used the blood samples, which contained DNA, for other unrelated studies. This included studies on taboo subjects to the tribe: schizophrenia, migration, and inbreeding. The Havasupai tribe filed a lawsuit against the Arizona Board of Regents and ASU researchers for misappropriation of their DNA samples. The legal process was lengthy and convoluted; the original case was dismissed. The Arizona Court of Appeals later reinstated the lawsuit, and after a prolonged legal battle, the matter was finally settled. The Havasupai people suffered greatly from the experience. The tribe suffered stigmatization when it was revealed that the "inbreeding coefficient" was high in comparison to other Native tribes. The information was communicated to the tribe inconsiderately, and it was interpreted that tribal members inbreed with each other. Not only was this not true, but inbreeding is forbidden, and this and other taboos are explicit for Havasupai people (Mello and Wolf 2010). The research experience of the Havasupai tribe is a distressing example of research protocols that did not incorporate the values and traditions of the people being researched.

The experience of the Havasupai people could have been so different had the tenets of gentle action theory been applied to the research project. First, a member of the research team who had gained the trust of the tribe could have been their cultural liaison. With the assistance of the cultural liaison the researchers could have participated in a series of Talking Circles. The Talking Circles would have aided the community and researchers to build trust and foster a relationship. The Elders and cultural liaison would have had the opportunity to share significant cultural norms and taboos that might have materialized while conducting their research.

The research process could then have been introduced and discussed. Tribal members could have expressed their concerns and asked clarifying questions. Since English was the second language for most the Havasupai people, the consent form could have been presented in many ways. At the outset, the form could have been co-created between the researchers and tribal members. This would have increased the understanding and buy-in to the research project. Issues of how the blood samples would be used could have been dealt with before any samples were taken. A transparent process with high ethical standards would have obliterated the problems that resulted from the way the process was handled.

A member of the tribe could have translated the form into the Havasupai language. The form could have been presented orally in both Havasupai and English. In addition, it is customary in Native American culture for an Elder or family spokesperson to accompany family members for medical based appointments, and had that been part of the process, that family leader could have helped to ensure that the research participant understood how their blood sample would be used. Throughout the entire process, gentle action would have helped to address the complexity and delicate nature of the tribal system by listening and learning about the needs, concerns, and parameters of the Havasupai people before embarking on the research project. Using this method, the harm would not have been done. Gentle action at its core reflects traditional ways of knowing and being found in Native American culture.

GENTLE ACTION THEORY AND THE CREE

Traditionally teachings of the Chippewa Cree were handed down orally and by the way one lived one's life. Stories told by leaders, Elders, and family members were and are told to provide cultural history, lessons, and examples of how Creator and the Ancestors desire us to be in this world and in the next. It is important to understand that the written Cree language was a result of the efforts of both Jesuit and Methodist missionaries. Fortunately for Cree people the language has not been lost; the highest numbers of Cree speakers are in Canada. There is a Cree immersion program at schools on the Rocky Boy's Reservation. Elders have been and continue to be recorded to preserve language and tribal history.

The legends of the Cree often provide lessons that demonstrate the parallels of traditional ways of knowing and being and gentle action theory. One such Cree legend is the legend of Crow and Little Bear. It is important to know that while the body of a story does not change when being told, the storyteller may embellish certain parts of the story. In addition, the story in its original form would have been oral.

CROW AND LITTLE BEAR

A long time ago, there was a crow who lived by a big river. It was a very big river, with a strong rushing current and fierce rapid. The river was full of fish, but the current was too fast for Crow to attempt fishing. If she fell in the river, she would be swept downstream. One morning, Crow awoke to find a little bear on the beach by the river. Little Bear was a stranger, and looked lost. Crow watched Little Bear curiously. Little Bear spent several days lying on the beach, watching Crow. Crow spent her time sitting in a big tree, dreaming about the fish she could catch and watching Little Bear.

One day, Little Bear was crying. Crow saw this, so she flew down to the beach to see what the problem was.

"Hello," said Crow.

"Hello," said Little Bear.

"I'm sorry I didn't introduce myself sooner. I am quite shy," said Crow.

"That's okay," said Little Bear. "I am shy, too."

"Why are you crying?" asked Crow.

"I miss my home," said Little Bear. "I'm not from this part of the woods."

Little Bear explained how he had arrived at this beach. One fine sunny day, his parents had gone fishing. Little Bear had wandered off to find an adventure. What he found was a big river. Little Bear thought he would catch a big fish and bring it home to impress his parents. But as soon as he took one step into the swirling rapids, he was swept away downstream. He would have drowned if he had not grabbed onto a log. The log carried him far down the river, for days and nights, until he came to rest on the beach.

"So, that is how I ended up here," said Little Bear. "And I miss my home because there is such good fishing there."

Ahh haa, thought Crow to herself. Good fishing! Crow was always eager to find easier ways of fishing.

"Why don't you go home?" asked Crow. It seemed like a pretty obvious question.

Little Bear shook his head vigorously. "Oh no! I will never set foot in that river again!" Little Bear sat down and began to cry again when he thought of all the good fishing at his home.

Crow sat quietly until Little Bear finished crying. "I think I can get you home," said Crow.

"How?" asked Little Bear eagerly? Little Bear was running around in circles, he was so excited.

"It would involve climbing some trees and rocks."

Little Bear fell onto his rump and started to cry again.

"What's the matter now?" asked Crow.

"My parents tried to teach me, but I was never very good at climbing trees or rocks," said Little Bear. "I don't know how."

Crow shook her head. "That's not the right attitude, friend. Let's go give it a try."

Crow and Little Bear walked toward the mountain. When they came to the first set of big rocks, Crow flew to the top and called down, "Come on up, Little Bear."

Little Bear jumped on the rock, and slid straight to the bottom. He jumped up and tried again, with the same result. Little Bear looked like he was about to cry again.

This could be harder than I thought, said Crow to herself.

Crow flew back to the beach, and filled her claws with sand. She spread the sand all over the rocks. "Try it now, Little Bear."

Little Bear shook his head. "No way," he said.

"It will be easier this time, Little Bear," said Crow. "I promise."

Little Bear hopped onto the rock, and to his surprise, he did not slide off. Slowly, he inched his way up the rock until he had reached the top. He and Crow celebrated. They began to make their way up the mountain, with Crow spreading sand on the rocks and Little Bear climbing inch by inch. By the time they reached the top, Crow was not using any sand at all.

"Congratulations," said Crow. "You did that quite well."

"My stomach is kind of sore," said Little Bear. "But I learned how to climb rocks!"

"You should never stop learning."

"I guess that is true."

They took a rest and gazed out at the scene. "I still can't see my home," said Little Bear.

Crow hopped onto the branch of a nearby tree. "If we climb up here, you will be able to see your home."

"I can't climb trees!" said Little Bear. Crow shook her head at him.

"Oh, okay. I'll try," sighed Little Bear.

Little Bear grabbed Crow's wing and hopped onto the first branch. He started to climb, but lost his hold and nearly fell out of the tree.

This could be harder than I thought, said Crow to herself.

"Little Bear, do you see this bark on the tree? Dig your claws into the bark. That is what you have claws for."

Little Bear was very scared. He tried digging his claws into the bark. To his surprise, he got a very good grip. Slowly, he became more confident in his claws, and he began to make his way up the tree. Crow hopped from branch to branch, encouraging him along the way. Finally, after a great deal of climbing, they reached the top of the tallest tree on the mountain. Little Bear was very excited.

"Thank you, Crow. Thank you for teaching me how to climb trees! And look, over there. There is my home!"

Crow looked to the lakes in the west where Little Bear was pointing. She could almost taste the fish.

"But how are we ever going to get from this tall tree to my home?" asked Little Bear.

"Little Bear, we are going to fly," said Crow.

"Crow, my friend, you have taught me quite a lot today. But I think you're getting a little carried away."

"Little Bear, trust me!" cried Crow. "Think of your home and all those tasty fish."

Bear closed his eyes and began daydreaming about all the fish in the lakes. As soon as he closed his eyes, Crow flapped her wing in the air and pushed Little Bear from the tree.

"Yooouuu puuusshed meeeeee!" yelled Little Bear as he fell through the sky, legs flailing in the air.

Suddenly, Crow swooped below him and caught him on her back. "Wrap your arms around my neck or you'll fall off," she said.

Little Bear did as he was told. The shock wore off and he realized that he was flying. "Hey, we're flying!"

Little Bear was enjoying the flight. He looked around at the trees and lakes and the big river far below.

Crow kept her wings outspread as Little Bear clutched onto her neck. They flew along the wind currents, rising and falling as they drifted to Little Bear's home. "Flying is pretty neat," said Little Bear.

"Yes, I guess I take it for granted," said Crow.

As they got closer to Little Bear's home, Crow was getting quite tired. "Little Bear, you are getting very heavy. I think we should land."

"Good idea, Crow. Take us by that lake. It is good fishing there."

Crow and Little Bear landed by the lake. Now that their long journey was over, they were hungry. Fish began jumping from the water in great numbers right in front of them.

"Look at all those fish!" exclaimed Crow. She grew so excited that she dove into the lake and began flapping around, trying to snap up fish in her beak. She splashed and spluttered, and did not catch one fish.

Little Bear began to laugh at his friend. "No wonder you are hungry all the time. Come here and dry off."

As Crow shook all her feathers, Little Bear crept to the shore of the lake. He knelt down and slipped his paw into the water. Little Bear began quietly to sing a song.

Crow watched Little Bear. He is taking an awfully long time, thought Crow to herself. Why is he just sitting there? I am getting hungry.

Suddenly, Little Bear scooped his paw and a large fish came flying out of the lake. Minutes later he repeated the action, and another fish landed on the shore. Little Bear turned to Crow and smiled. "That should be enough for dinner. We don't need any more."

The two friends had a meal of fish. "My father taught me that it is important to sing that song when I go fishing. It makes the fish sleepy," said Little Bear.

"Well, it is a much better way of fishing than my method," laughed Crow.

They ate most of the fish, and wrapped the rest as a gift for Little Bear's people. The pair travelled to Little Bear's home. Little Bear's people were overjoyed to see him again and they threw a huge feast for Crow. Crow was happy with Little Bear's people and the good fishing in the lake, so she decided to stay. She never went back to the big river again. (Harvey McCue and Associates 2010, 28–34)

The legend of Crow and Little Bear is illustrative of gentle action theory and traditional ways of knowing and being in several ways. The first example is in the way in which Crow and Little Bear first met each other. Crow watched Little Bear with curiosity while Little Bear in turn spent days watching Crow. They did not jump into conversation and instead observed each other while thinking about their individual situations, allowing themselves the creative suspension as found in gentle action theory. Like in gentle action theory, there was an allowance of time and space between the Crow and Little Bear.

Next Crow responded to the crying of Little Bear while apologizing for her lack of manners and disclosing personal information about her own shyness. Little Bear excused the behavior and shared that he too was shy, therefore building rapport between them. Crow respectfully asked Little Bear why he was crying and, when Little Bear responded that he missed his home, Crow felt empowered to inquire why Little Bear didn't just go home. Little Bear goes on to share how he had gotten into the situation and his fears about the river. The legend exhibits the need for listening and learning, allowing Crow to understand the situation, while learning more about Little Bear and his home, including the good fishing that was to be had there.

Crow waited quietly for Little Bear to finish crying. She did not jump in with a solution, admonishment, or try and take control of the situation which is the approach of gentle action theory. Crow felt that she could help Little Bear go home. She offered gentle advice, encouragement, and offered to problem solve with Little Bear. Crow was aware of her own energy and capacity so that she was able to be honest that she was tired as Little Bear was heavy and suggested that it would be wise to land. Instead of pushing Crow beyond her limit, Little Bear saw the wisdom in landing and suggested landing by the lake, where they could both gain sustenance from the fish found there. This demonstrates the mutuality that gentle action seeks in relationships and problem solving.

Crow dove right in, anxious to catch a fish, with no success. She watched as Little Bear took his time, singing, and slipping his paw into the water. Little Bear successfully caught two fish for himself and Crow. Little Bear shared that his father taught him always to sing the song when he fished as it puts the fish to sleep. Crow gained dinner and knowledge about the cultural tradition of Little Bear's family and fishing. The two wrapped up fish for Little Bear's people instead of eating it all up themselves. Gifting is a tradition in Native American culture when one returns home. It also demonstrates selflessness. Crow enjoyed and liked Little Bear's people, deciding to stay and be part of the community. Gentle action theory is about building community, while problem solving, while acting with sensitivity, establishing trust, and seeking harmony; all aspects which are evident in the legend of Crow and Little Bear.

Teaching and presenting workshops, I have found that students/learners are open to hearing about theory if they can perceive the practical application of the theory. Preparing for the Healing the Sacred Hoop workshop, I wanted to be able to impart the concepts of gentle action theory in a manner people could apply to their current situation and especially to the time when they would be released and go back home and back into community.

WHOLE SYSTEMS HEALING

The University of Minnesota's Earl E. Bakken Center for Spirituality and Healing offers inter-professional education, conducts rigorous research, delivers innovative engagement programs, and advances innovative models of care. John Miller, MAE, and F. David Peat, PhD, offer a gentle action learning module as members of the whole systems healing collaborators. In conducting the Healing the Sacred Hoop workshop at CCCF, I utilized the examples and nonexamples of gentle action as outlined in the section, "Building a Basis for Action." (See table 1.)

Working with the women, gentle action was an approach that they had not experienced. First, colonization has permeated our culture, our systems, our identities, and our way of being in the world. Second, the women have spent their lives in systems and institutions not designed for them. These include school, foster care, organized religion, and the prison itself. The women operated from within the conditioning of these experiences coupled with their own trauma, resulting in both a lack of critical thinking skills and an inability to envision a different life for themselves.

The first question I asked them was, "What would you like to do when you get out of here?" All of them said, "I'm not coming back here," but when I asked, "How will you make sure that you don't reoffend?" they did not have specific ways to make sure they would change their

Table 1. Gentle Action: A Better Way—Building a Basis for Action

TYPICAL APPROACH	GENTLE ACTION APPROACH
Change others	*Change ourselves*
We try to bring about change from the outside. In doing so, we focus on trying to change others . . .	. . . rather than realizing that true change begins at home. Gandhi said, "Be the change." This means that we can only bring change to a system of which we are (or we become) an integral part.
Act from a limited perspective	*Act from a comprehensive picture*
We tend to see things from a limited perspective (our own), then try to get others to see them our way and enlist allies to move our own agendas.	Even when we are part of a system, our perspectives are bound to be limited. To understand all aspects of the system more fully, we need to listen to a variety of other perspectives, then work with others to build a comprehensive picture.
Focus on what's wrong	*Focus on what's right*
We tend to focus more on what's wrong with a system and how we're going to fix it than on understanding how the system actually works.	By immersing ourselves deeply in the workings of the system, we can see what's working well. This helps us think of ways to subtly redirect energies, refine processes, and readjust relationships, to achieve helpful changes with minimal disruption.
Wait until we're certain	*Embrace uncertainty*
We may not want to proceed because we can never have complete information about a complex system or how it will respond to change.	Even as we try to build a thorough understanding of how the system works, we need to become more comfortable with the fact that complete knowledge is unattainable. We can't afford to allow uncertainty to prevent us from acting.

Source: Written by John Miller, MAE, and F. David Peat, PhD. © 2009 Regents of the University of Minnesota. All rights reserved. Reprinted with permission from Earl E. Bakken Center for Spirituality and Healing, University of Minnesota.

Table 2. Gentle Action Approach — Taking Action

TYPICAL APPROACH	GENTLE ACTION APPROACH
Use central power	*Use grassroots actions*
We equate power and control with change, so we try to bring lots of power to address big issues.	But complex systems typically change as the result of small, frequent influences over time. When we recognize this, we realize that even widespread or obstinate problems are within our collective reach.
Go for one solution	*Choose many small actions*
We go for a single solution — one big hammer or magic bullet that will make radical change.	But a complex system depends on many small parts, functioning intricately together. By working in many complementary ways, we can influence multiple aspects or levels of the system at the same time.
Stick to definitive plans	*Respond flexibly*
We make detailed, definitive plans and think we have to stick to them at all costs.	But complex systems are inherently unpredictable — we can't know how they'll respond to our actions. So as we proceed we have to watch carefully to see how our actions are affecting the system, making continual adjustments to our plans as we go along.
Expect a dramatic response	*Watch patiently for little signs of change*
When we don't see the system changing according to our input, we get discouraged and give up prematurely.	Complex systems can be highly resilient and resistant to change. Often a system stays in equilibrium until a "tipping point" is reached. Our actions may seem like they are having no effect. But once critical momentum is achieved, deep-seated changes take root and begin to spread. Understanding this, we'll be less likely to give up when, in fact, success may simply be a matter of sustained effort over time.

Source: Written by John Miller, MAE, and F. David Peat, PhD. © 2009 Regents of the University of Minnesota and Life Science Foundation. All rights reserved. Reprinted with permission from Earl E. Bakken Center for Spirituality and Healing, University of Minnesota.

situations and lives. The Western approach is a hard-nosed one where these women might hear things like, "Well, what are you going to do about it?" "You've been incarcerated multiple times or most of your life, your odds aren't good," and "Leopards don't change their spots." Throughout the time we spent together, we used the examples and non-examples of gentle action to address their life issues and examine the past to imagine a different life for them. This method not only helped the women create life plans for after prison; it provided essential tools to cope with life inside the prison.

MISTY (NATIVE AMERICAN, AFRICAN AMERICAN, AND WHITE)
I first met Misty when she was incarcerated at the Coffee Creek Correctional Facility. Misty was a participant in the Healing the Sacred Hoop workshop. After her release she became one of the women in my circle of mentoring. She and I have an ongoing relationship of mentoring and friendship. Misty has graciously chosen to share her some of her story.

Misty was twenty-three years old when she was first incarcerated in 2003. She was released in 2009 and then returned in 2009 until 2013. Her first charge in 2003 was a second-degree robbery with a firearm and her second charge was a third-degree robbery, which means that in the course of committing or attempting to commit theft or unauthorized use of a vehicle the person uses or threatens the immediate use of physical force upon another person. Misty says, "Prison was rough for sure . . . being away from my family and kids and losing my grandmother while being there are some of the hardest things I have ever had to do. Being so young and growing up there . . . I [had a] hard time for a long time and didn't make the best choices my entire first time incarcerated. I continued those bad behaviors upon release and went right back to prison in the first three months after I was released. My second time . . . something clicked, and I knew I had to decide if I wanted better or if I wanted to continue a path to destruction." We will return to Misty's story later.

Throughout the Healing the Sacred Hoop workshop at CCCF, we discussed and examined both the women's life experiences and their own self-assessment of what brought them to prison. I utilized the examples and nonexamples of gentle action as they began to create their individual action plans for their lives upon release from prison.

Key to applying gentle action throughout the workshop was the understanding of and respect for the women's lived experience as well as their cultural belief systems. Equally important was the method of delivery. Kindness, respect, dignity, empathy, and lack of judgment were core to building trust and relationship between myself and the women; and between the women and each other. This model of the way of being connected through gentle action and traditional ways became both educational and empowering for the women.

Gentle action theory correlates well with the tenets of traditional ways of knowing and being, and for me as a Cree person, they resonate with what I have been taught. There are core aspects of traditional ways that can be considered cultural norms across tribes. However, tribal belief systems vary from tribe to tribe and are in direct relation to place and tribal histories. Traditional ways of knowing, being, and learning are central to Native American culture. The cosmology of the Cree is discussed later.

CHAPTER 6

Cree Traditional Justice

There is no one size that fits all in describing the traditional justice systems of the First Nations People of Canada. However, the Aboriginal Justice Implementation Commission (AJIC), created in November 1999 in Canada, offers an excellent précis of traditional justice and its meanings. Please note that although the commission uses the term Aboriginal, in contemporary times, the term most used and accepted is First Nations people. According to its website, the commission's purpose was "to develop an action plan based on the original Aboriginal Justice Inquiry recommendations" in response to two incidents where Aboriginal citizens were unhappy with the way the incidents were handled by law enforcement and the court. A portion of the work of the AJIC was focused on community and restorative justice in relation to the Aboriginal people of Canada (AJIC, n.d.).

The AJIC provided their working definition of the purpose of a system of traditional justice for the Aboriginal people of Canada as follows: "The purpose of a justice system in an Aboriginal society is to restore the peace and equilibrium within the community, and to reconcile the accused with his or her own conscience and with the individual or family who has been wronged. This is a primary difference between the dominant society and Aboriginal people. It is a difference that significantly challenges the appropriateness of the present legal and justice system for Aboriginal people in the resolution of conflict, the reconciliation and the maintenance of community harmony and good order" (AJIC 2001).

The AJIC provided their working definition of the meaning of justice for the Aboriginal people of Canada in terms of traditional justice: "At the most basic level of understanding, justice is understood differently by Aboriginal people. The dominant society tries to control actions it considers potentially harmful to society, to individuals or to the wrong-doers themselves by interdiction, enforcement or apprehension, in order to prevent or punish harmful or deviant behavior. The emphasis is on the punishment of the deviant as a means of making that person conform, or as a means of protecting other members of society" (AJIC 2001).

ABORIGINAL CONCEPTS OF LAW

The AJIC stresses that, contrary to the understanding of some people outside the culture, there were and are Aboriginal laws. Furthermore, the AJIC recognizes on its website that there were and will continue to be Aboriginal governments with the power to make laws and the systems to enforce those laws. Aboriginal people have constitutions that are the supreme "law of laws" for their nations and peoples. Societies cannot function without law. The systems of law and order grow from the beliefs, customs, traditions, and rules of a society of people. The societal norms shaped what the group considered to be acceptable and unacceptable behavior. Each nation had a form of meting out justice.

Traditional courts of justice focused primarily on restoring balance between the wrongdoer, the individual or families harmed, and ultimately the community. A common practice would have the wrongdoer and that individual's family going before the community, community leadership such as a chief or chiefs and group of Elders, along with the person or persons who were harmed, who would also have their family with them. The person causing harm and the person or persons experiencing the harm would share their story of the event. Those present could ask clarifying questions and could object to any part of the telling that they found nonfactual. The individual and family who experienced the harm could ask for the compensation that they felt was appropriate. The leadership and Elders could offer terms of compensation to the individual or family harmed. Negotiation between the parties was possible until compensation was agreed upon. Two key elements of the process were (a) that the wrongdoer admitted and accepted responsibility for the actions, and (b) unlike in Western justice systems, there was an understanding that one cannot be made "whole"; rather there is healing and reunification between the parties involved, as well as the entire community, but there is a recognition that the person harmed and the community have been changed by the act of the perpetrator (AJIC 2001).

The AJIC outlined some of the common elements of an Aboriginal traditional justice system for the Aboriginal people of Canada:

There were laws against certain types of behaviors.

The types of behaviors which were objectionable or aberrant varied from those of European societies.

Sanctions were imposed differently than European societies.

Social control rested in kinship.

Sanctions included ridicule, shaming, and avoidance of community members whose behavior harmed an individual or the group.

Compensation and reparation took many forms depending on the level of harm and was the responsibility of both the offender and the family of the offender.

Societal rank, gender, and the age of the person harmed was taken into consideration. The compensation for a crime against a chief or an Elder could possibly be greater than that paid to a person of lower rank. The compensation for a crime against a woman or child could be greater than that against a man.

Crimes such as murder or repeated deviant behavior against a person and especially a child often resulted in banishment.

Murder was dealt with by each Nation in its own way. However, the preferred norm was a system of atonement and reparation by the offender to the victim's family. The payment would be borne by all members of the offender's kinship group and would be shared by all members of the victim's kinship group. In theory, the family which was harmed had the right to resort to violence either through a blood feud between the families or the slaying of either the murderer or someone closely related to him. There was not capital punishment as found in European societies. (AJIC 2001)

ABORIGINAL PEOPLE AND THE ROLE OF THE ELDERS

The AJIC (2001) emphasizes that Elders, both men and women, have always been central in traditional justice systems for the Aboriginal people of Canada. Elders are teachers, healers, and carriers of culture. Before contact with colonizers there was no written language, knowledge was shared via oral tradition, and practices were passed on by the Elders of a community. Elders were and are respected for their knowledge, their lived experiences, and their wisdom. Elders were and are sought out for their advice.

The AJIC (2001) aptly describes an Aboriginal belief system as being one in which each person has three aspects that make up his or her whole being: the body, the mind, and the spirit. The belief system is that for Aboriginal people to heal, all aspects of their being need to be treated. In the case of Aboriginal inmates, Elders believe that healing is required for them because of what led them to perpetrate the crime and because the experience of incarceration is harmful to one's mind and spirit.

Patricia Monture, in the chapter "Women and Risk," one of her contributions to the book *First Voices: An Aboriginal Women's Reader* (Monture and McGuire 2009), offers her opinion that a large gap still remains between Aboriginal understandings of the justice struggles they experience and the plethora of reports put forth by the Royal Commission on Aboriginal Peoples. She is most troubled that the report is silent on how to rectify the negative experiences of Aboriginal women in prison. She cites the fact that Aboriginal women are incarcerated at a higher representative number than Aboriginal men, creating a double silence by the Royal Commission. Monture asserts that this is of great consequence as the sentencing and prison experiences of Aboriginal women prisoners are often based on the denial of gender as well as race and culture (Monture 2009).

Monture has served as a member of the Task Force on Federally Sentenced Women and feels that many of her contributions and values have been profoundly disrespected by the Correctional Service of Canada.

She sees the Aboriginal visioning done by First Nations people and communities as being ignored and invisible under the systematic federal bureaucracy. Monture states, "The conclusion is that one of the foundational ideas of current correctional policy is, in my opinion, incompatible with Aboriginal cultures, laws, and traditions" (Monture 2009, 418). She emphasizes that enough research has been done to substantiate the devastating effects that the Canadian criminal justice system has had on both Aboriginal people and the First Nations communities, with not enough work being done to remedy the situation. Monture (2009) feels it is time to revisit the work of the task force and design a project with formal structure while focusing on the original vision. Monture found that the task force was unmindful of the systematic assessment tools utilized to classify federally sentenced women as a whole and that the classification instruments put women, particularly culturally, racially, and cognitively marginalized women, at a disadvantage. She asserts that the task force, which was formed to survey all federally sentenced women in Canada and provide recommendations for the future of women's corrections needs, should consider the policies more deeply in terms of Aboriginal women, both in theory and in practical application.

CONTEMPORARY JUDICIAL SYSTEM AT ROCKY BOY'S INDIAN RESERVATION

Living away from Rocky Boy, I do not have personal knowledge or experience as to the workings of the judicial system there. However, my niece, Judge Melody Whitford (Chippewa), was kind enough to do a personal interview with me. Through her I was able to get a sense of how the court operates and the cultural aspects of the Chippewa Cree people within the contemporary tribal justice system (Whitford 2016).

The court system does allow individuals to hire attorneys, and/or use the public defender, which is required under the Indian Bill of Rights. There is currently one court-appointed attorney, and in addition there is a local agency, Montana Legal Services, that offers legal assistance to those who qualify. The detention center can hold up to seventy-five people. There is a juvenile wing in the current detention center; however, it is not used because the tribe does not have the funding to maintain it.

Juveniles are sent to Busby, Montana, which is a five-hour drive away from Rocky Boy. Judges at one point in time were elected; however, due to corruption, including one former judge being sentenced to federal prison after alerting drug dealers about a search warrant, the tribe began to appoint them. The term of appointment started at one year and more recently expanded to two-year terms in 2014 (Whitford 2016).

All major cases, including capital cases, rape, murder, kidnapping, embezzling, and so forth, can be heard in both Federal Court and Tribal Court. Typically, defendants are charged in Tribal Court to get them off the streets and to allow the federal government time to prepare their case. Once the case has been prepared, the defendant is typically moved to a federal facility after appearing before a federal judge. Judge Whitford articulated that it does get interesting because now tribes have the right to seek enhanced sentencing under the Tribal Law and Order Act (TOLA). The Chippewa Cree Tribe does not have the financial resources to do so. Elders are used for customary adoptions only. They do utilize Tribal Peacekeepers but again only for civil matters and mainly for adoption proceedings. There is not currently prayer before court proceedings; however, Judge Whitford thinks that is a great idea and may implement it in her courtroom (Whitford 2016).

It is not easy being a tribal judge. The cases that come before judges often involve family members. Tribal life and, in particular, reservation life means that you are surrounded by relatives. Those relatives may come from your father's side, or your mother's side, or be relatives of your spouse. Aunts, uncles, cousins, nieces, and nephews from three generations live at Rocky Boy, and it is 100 percent guaranteed that family will come before the court. People may be angry at the decisions made, sentences rendered, and fines levied (Whitford 2016).

Judge Whitford connected me with Kirstin Russell (Chippewa Cree), who is the clerk of court supervisor, deputy clerk, at Rocky Boy. The responsibilities of Ms. Russell's position include the receipt and examination of legal documents for accuracy, completeness, and adherence to requirements. She prepares and maintains documents and exhibits; files legal documents and related case materials; retrieves and delivers files and documents to court or appropriate parties; and maintains court records and files. In her role she advises attorneys, agencies, and the public on the status of cases in a professional and courteous manner; provides procedural information; answers inquiries and explains filing processes; explains fees and fines; and assists individuals in locating material and information. She issues legal documents, such as warrants, writs, subpoenas, abstracts, and other official documents, on behalf of the court in accordance with policies and procedures, recalls warrants, exonerates bail, prepares judgments, and dismisses or seals cases in accordance with established codes and court procedures. She accepts fines and fees, and maintains and updates financial records. She prepares court calendars and schedules cases for hearings, conferring with the appropriate individuals per established procedures, and distributes calendars and related case files (Russell 2016).

Ms. Russell shared that the court has what is called an Elders Panel. When there is a customary adoption and the adopting parents request it, they have the Elders Panel sit in on the adoption. The Elders offer prayers, advice, and good words to the adoptive parents. Elders counsel clients of the court. Participants in the court programs are also required to participate in cultural teachings with tribal Elders. Ms. Russell shared that they do have staff that smudge and pray before the day starts and do utilize Elders. She is fairly new to implementing traditional ways into their department. She loves being a public servant. Knowing that she plays a part in helping her community is truly rewarding for her. She is acknowledged for her level of professionalism and empathy to her people and finds that to be amazing. There are challenges. There are times when the court cannot assist everyone, or they are unhappy with the outcome of a case and their anger is directed at her or her clerks. It becomes hard at times to be able to soothe that anger and know the proper way to deescalate the situation that leaves everyone with peace of mind. Also, when they have clients in their Adult Healing to Wellness program who relapse or regress, she feels their frustration and disappointment. She cites her downfall as becoming overinvolved with her cases while wanting nothing more than for clients to succeed. Their triumphs are shared triumphs. Their downfalls are shared downfalls (Russell 2016).

Traditional justice systems are a representation of gentle action theory applied practically in both historical and contemporary times. Traditional justice systems come from within a society and are applied in a manner that the society can agree with and accept. The focus and purpose of traditional justice systems juxtapose well with gentle action theory in that the desired outcome is not about winning or losing. Rather, the desired outcome is one of bringing balance, healing, and restoration to the person committing the harm, to the person and family that has been harmed, and to the community.

Western justice is different in that it is both adversarial and punitive. Western justice has a concept of "make whole." It is a term used in reference to compensating a party for a loss sustained. The precise definition varies according to contract terms and local laws. It may include either actual economic losses or may extend to noneconomic losses, and may not necessarily apply only to the settlement value of the case. Traditional justice systems do not operate from that premise. For example, if someone murders a member of my family, my life would never be the same, and no punishment could make me whole. Rather, in traditional ways, all involved would come together to determine what actions need to be taken.

It is gratifying to see that the First Nations Cree of Canada have not lost the model of traditional justice systems long practiced by their people. One can comprehend the differences between the dominant systems of Canada and the United States experienced by First Nations people and Native Americans by looking at the comparison between the system in place at Rocky Boy and that outlined by the AJIC.

The Chippewa Cree of Rocky Boy have implemented some traditional ways of justice and are intent on increasing the use of traditional ways. I appreciated the honesty of Judge Whitford regarding the corruption and criminal activity that the tribe has experienced in recent and not so recent times. Unfortunately, across the tribes of the United States, such barriers to ethical justice are not limited to the Chippewa Cree of Rocky Boy. On a positive note, many tribes are reclaiming systems of traditional justice.

CHAPTER 7

Narratives of Incarceration and Healing

The Healing the Sacred Hoop workshop was a special experience for the women who participated. I asked some of the women who were either in the workshop or whom I have mentored while applying gentle action theory to share their feelings about having access to Native American spirtual services during or after their incarceration. Included are responses from the wrap-up interview questions from workshop participants at the conclusion of our time together. Reading and processing the responses of the women in their own words, from their perspective, both informed me of the validity of employing gentle action theory and created an opportunity for me to reflect on how I will use gentle action theory in my work moving forward.

RETURNING TO MYRNA'S STORY (CHAPTER 1)

"I heard about spiritual services for Native women from one of the Native women in prison. She kept telling me that I needed to go with her to sweat. I finally decided to go because I was at the point where I was ready to take my own life. When I first began to go to sweat, the area was just a little piece of dirt full of stickers. Those stickers were the most profound thing that had ever happened to me. And going to sweat saved me. I would think about those stickers and that time in sweat. That whole month after sweat, before the next month's sweat; I would think about my prayers, that feeling, that cleansing.

That feeling of being human. You don't feel human when you're in prison at all. I was also able to go to talking circle about once a month and being with the other Native women and building community inside the prison was healing for me." The younger women looked to Myrna for support and leadership. She drew on her experience as a homemaker, a mom, and nurturer. Taking part in sweat, talking circle, and the First Foods Feast made her feel normal. Myrna says, "The gift of people coming in and teaching you about ceremony makes you feel whole." She articulated, "I wouldn't have survived without the ceremony, without the prayers, Tyler giving me my prayer feather was especially important to me. Ceremony and acceptance helped with my healing. Before prison, I was ashamed, because I was light skinned and didn't have a tribal card; I didn't feel Indian enough. I didn't know about ceremony, how to properly do things, and was afraid of making a misstep. There was a hole in my spirit. Being able to gain the knowledge and spiritual experience has brought me to fortifying my sense of being that I am a Native woman, my identity, my spiritual being; and no one can take that away from me."

By the time I met Myrna, she was nearing the end of her sentence. She had become a leader and mentor within the Native American women's spiritual circle. Her inclusiveness, grace, and kind heart were characteristics that the women really needed. Upon her release Myrna brought those things to the Native community in Oregon. She is a passionate supporter for both women and men who are behind bars and those who have transitioned out to community. Despite health problems and the cares of everyday living, including financial insecurity and a need for a steady home, Myrna is serving, mentoring, advocating, and bringing spiritual services to her people.

RETURNING TO MISTY'S STORY (CHAPTER 5)
"Being able to connect with Red Lodge volunteers and having support through ceremony, services, classes, and workshops not only helped me rid myself of generational curses, it also gave me so much of what I needed to succeed. It was a lot of work, learning how to be a productive member of society. But I can proudly say that I just celebrated seven years free, and I honestly met a few women there I would not trade for the world. Prison is what you make of it."

Today Misty holds a management position at her job and has received Employee of the Month numerous times. She achieved a dream when she reunited with her husband and daughter, and they added another daughter to their family. Her family is the center of her life. Misty has maintained healthy relationships with women she was close to in prison. Misty did the difficult self-work both in the Healing the Sacred Hoop workshop and when she paroled out, and it has resulted in her creating the life she wanted and thought she might not ever have.

RETURNING TO BRANDIE'S STORY (CHAPTER 4)

Taking part in spiritual services and programming was meaningful for Brandie. She says, "It felt like freedom when I was able to attend talking circles, sweat lodge, and the spring celebration. For the time we were able to gather together for events it gave me a sense of freedom and comfort. We were able to talk, laugh, hug, and be together without being under the watchful eye of officers and other inmates." She expressed that without spiritual programming she would have felt "frustration by not being able to be ourselves and not having a place to be together."

Brandie has stayed sober since 2015. She has a relationship with her kids, and she says, "I'm showing them that they can count on me now." She cannot take things back that happened, but she and her children can build a new life together. Brandie added another daughter to her family. Brandie is in school and working on a certificate in addiction studies.

RETURNING TO BARBARA'S STORY (CHAPTER 1)

Barbara shared that when she got to CCCF she did not participate in the Native American cultural programs. She felt she was a bad person and not good enough to participate. Prison made her understand how different she was as a Native woman, in an institution created by white people. Barbara was strong of opinion and action and was not one to stand down to authority. She became branded as a "bad guy" and a troublemaker. She felt like she was always in trouble for being herself.

She saw a lot of brokenness in the Native sisters. Barbara did not like being treated disrespectfully for being a strong person. She stood up for her Native sisters. The guards called her a leader, an instigator, and a shot caller. The officers preached at her for being a leader, and even the prison superintendent came to see her when Barbara was in segregation. Barbara did not mind being in segregation because it got her away from the chaos and racism on the unit. They threatened to move Barbara out of state, which would have resulted in her being away from her family.

Barbara realized that she had been incarcerated during crucial years of her life. As she described, most teenagers and young adults "rip and run," maturing and learning on the outside. She "ripped and ran" in prison, and the system does not teach you about self-worth, self-love, or healthy relationships. Instead, you learn to trust no one in the system. You learn about the absolute power they have over you. You learn about abject racism and cruelty.

Two of the community members coming in to provide spiritual services, Tawna and Trish, kept reaching out, and Barbara began going to sweat and talking circle. Barbara was selected to be part of the Healing the Sacred Hoop workshop. She had not previously experienced the model of gentle action theory.

Barbara felt empowered, and being part of the group provided her a sense of belonging. She found it to be a place where she was respected. It became a place that she could both honor and be honored. She found that her natural leadership skills became focused on standing up for things she believed in as a Native sister to be more meaningful. She felt like a human, not just an inmate or branded person. The workshop provided her with a different kind of freedom, and she craved more of that feeling. Barbara found meaning in standing up for the things she believed in, and it brought her personal power, even as a prisoner. She developed a deeper sense of self and her own sacredness as a Native woman. Leaning more about and practicing Native spirituality brought a deeper meaning of self and her role as a Native American woman.

Barbara appreciated all the community partners, Elders, and spiritual leaders who came in week after week. She and the other participants knew the days and times we would be there, and they looked forward to each session. Barbara valued our consistency and commitment and how we never let them down. "You were there for us!" she said, and that was something she and many of the other women had not previously experienced.

When we talked about what prison is like for Native American women, Barbara spoke of the lack of both services and Native staff. She was frustrated that Judeo-Christian services and programs happened daily or weekly while special sacred ceremonies for Native women were only held once a year. The Native women looked forward to and prepared for the First Foods Feast held each spring. But it was and is frustrating that the Department of Corrections does not acknowledge that there are many more special times of ceremony. Barbara expressed that there are few or no Native officers, teachers, chaplains, nurses, counselors, or program staff. She and the other women felt that workshop time became so sacred because "we don't get to see other faces like ours unless they are inmates."

Barbara said, "I wanted to have that impact that you had on all of us." She expressed that she and the other group members were watching us closely, and they wanted more of what we were modeling and to spend more time with us: "We wanted to be more like you." Barbara wanted to have the impact on others that we had on them. I am beyond honored and humbled by her saying, "You are our inspiration."

Barbara taught me so much. One of my clearest memories is a valuable life lesson I received from her. We were doing a check-in circle after one of the Healing the Sacred Hoop workshop evenings. When it got to Barbara's turn to share, she said, "People are always telling us things like 'You need to walk the Red Road,' and 'You need to honor your sacredness as a woman,' and other things about being Native women. How are we supposed to know these things?" It was a huge "ah ha" moment for me. Her comments caused me to step back and think about what she had to say, her feelings, as well as the feelings and experiences of the rest of the women in the group, in acknowledging that not all of them have had a role model to teach them those concepts.

The first lesson I gained from the experience was that I needed to address my own assumptions about the life experiences of the women. In doing so, I recognized three major concepts that I needed to take into consideration in working with all Native people in my circle of association, not just the Native women in the workshop:

(1) The idea that all Native people have had access to Elders, ceremony, and teachings.

(2) The idea that all Native people have had knowledge presented to them in such a manner that their minds and souls can receive it.

(3) The idea that these Native women have wanted to learn about and participate in the traditions and spiritual practices of their people.

Pondering these concepts and the lessons I needed to learn as a Native woman, leader, teacher, community member, activist, tribal member, and relative, and taking those lessons to heart, resulted in necessary self-growth. I then took those lessons and pondered the precepts of gentle action theory. I realized that as a practitioner and proponent of the theory I needed to pause, to listen, and to learn more about the systems that I am a part of as a Native American.

HEALING THE SACRED HOOP WRAP-UP
INTERVIEW QUESTIONS AND RESPONSES

At the conclusion of our time together in the workshop I asked the women a set of questions. The questions were designed to gain knowledge from them about their experience and feelings about the workshop, our time together, and their personal responses to the workshop and its themes as well as their own spirituality.

What has being in the Healing the Sacred Hoop workshop meant to you?
Healing Circle has taken me away from prison when we are all together. When we have visitors, I feel like I'm with family.

I enjoy every time we get together. It's our time to bond as women and Natives.

I really look forward to coming to the circle. It's good medicine to hear the words being spoken. Thank you for making me feel worthwhile.

I have missed my spiritual connections and I feel the Healing Circle is just that. It's one of the most positive and encouraging groups I attend, and I always leave better than when I came in.

I would like to share that I am grateful to have Healing Circle. It helps me to become more confident, connected, more understanding while having the chance to share and listen to others.

I looked forward to each and every class. I've grown closer to Creator and I appreciate all the time spent to give us this opportunity.

I really appreciate the time of those coming in. I have grown so much spiritually but have a long way to go.

I'm very grateful for this class. We don't have much support for our culture in here.

I was humbled to learn and take a look at myself as a student and as an Elder.

I really like that we spent time together and I learned a lot.

I liked this because I learned a lot about myself and realized a lot about others.

The knowledge that I took into my spirit from each of the speakers and sisters' words will help me to be stronger in the world.

REALITY CHECK / SUCCESS RATE

The work that I have done in leading the Healing the Sacred Hoop workshop, and as a mentor, professor, and program director, and all of my work in Indian Country, has never been about quantifying the work. Rather, it has been, and still is, about providing mentorship, advocacy, and teaching in a manner that fits my preferred way of being in the world as a Native American woman. More importantly it will always be about following traditional ways and being the community member that Creator and the Ancestors expect of me.

Therefore, I do not have "numbers" or "data" that prove or disprove success or failure of the practice of gentle action theory, and it was never my intention to do so. What I do have is an understanding of how the women who were in the workshop and my mentoring circle have fared since then. Ten of the twelve women had previously been incarcerated prior to being participants in the workshop. Of the original twelve women who participated in the first workshop, eight women are out of prison and have not re-offended. Two of the twelve were still in prison with release dates in 2021. One woman died in prison. She was serving a life sentence. One woman re-offended but is now out of prison. This information does not demonstrate anything other than if they are imprisoned; there was no embedded goal related to recidivism. The objective of the workshop was to provide cultural information, connection to community, and spiritual tools to provide further healing. Certainly, a positive corollary to the workshop experience would be decreasing recidivism.

Most of the women are doing well. Many of them have reunited with their children. Some have reunited with a spouse or gone on to marry or entered a partnership. Five women have added children to their families either by adoption or birth. Many of the women have some stability in their lives. There are many challenges in their lives, from abusive relationships to housing needs and the need for living-wage employment. Their biggest need is the never-ending necessity for cultural and community connection and support from their families and from the Native community, be it their tribal community or the Native community where they are now living. Healing does not occur overnight but takes an ongoing commitment. They need healthy Native elders, spiritual leaders, and friends and family. They need programs, support groups, advocates, mentors, and ethical service providers.

REFLECTIONS ON APPLYING GENTLE ACTION THEORY IN THE HEALING THE SACRED HOOP WORKSHOP AND AS A MENTOR

Gentle action theory offered me an opportunity to model a different way of being in the world for the women in the workshop as well as those in my mentoring circle. It also helped me to deal with the complexity of the issue and my own ways of interacting and problem solving. We are all influenced by our culture, our belief systems, and our life experiences. My experience of being taken from my family, being a foster child, and then being an adopted child has resulted in many layers of socialization. I was drawn to the issue of incarceration because of the incarceration of my brothers, nephews, and nieces. I wanted to serve Native women experiencing incarceration as a way to serve my own family, my tribe, and Indian Country, and I wanted to serve in a manner directed by Creator and the Ancestors. Gentle action theory helped me to analyze my beliefs, where they come from, how they form my patterns of communication, and how I conduct myself.

Peat (2008) states, "Natural and social systems can be enormously complex and subtle, and they can exhibit markedly different forms of behavior in different regions or contexts" (49). This concept is applicable to human systems and how we behave in those systems. In my life I have been involved in rigid systems. This was especially true when I worked for a mega corporation, which valued competition, high earnings, and uniformity of policy and personnel. I come from a culture which believes that some things in our lives are innate. We believe that those things are in our DNA and that they are passed down by our ancestors. I have lived in systems that are binary; where right is right, and wrong is wrong, and free will is limited by the societal norms of the larger Western culture, and I have struggled with those systems in all aspects of my life. Fortunately, long before beginning my dissertation and work with Native women experiencing incarceration, I had done a lot of self-work on my own sense of identity, my culture, my family history, and my preferred way of being in the world.

One of the tenets of gentle action theory is flexibility. Peat (2008) states, "A rigid system may have strength and resistance but is unable to give and yield" (73). The principle parallels well with traditional ways. Our ancestors lived in an environment that was not stagnant, resulting in their need to be flexible to respond to the needs of our people. Working with Native women who have experienced trauma and crisis (and who continue to experience these things) requires flexibility. Each person has different circumstances and needs, meaning there is no set formula that can be applied. As Peat (2008) states, "The spectrum from rigidity to flexibility not only operates within an organization but at the level of the individual" (79).

I have witnessed people and social service programs make exclusionary decisions about whom to serve. Terms such as "program ready" and "far enough along" are both pejorative and oppressive. Some of the Native women have expressed to me experiences both of not being offered services and of receiving services that were horrible and abusive. Women spoke of providers who were vindictive and revengeful, resulting in additional trauma. These types of experiences do not further healing, nor do they follow traditional ways of meeting the needs of our people. I hearken back to Barbara's comment that the women are being told that they should not only know about the healing they need but should already be there to be deemed worthy. All women who seek healing and hope are worthy of services.

We all utilize perceptions in our walk through life, and often those perceptions are incomplete or wrong. Peat (2008) declares: "So our ability to judge a situation, or make an intervention, is going to depend on the way we 'see' that situation" (82). That also applies to the way we "see" people. As discussed in chapter 5, Peat tells us, "The more we are aware of our prejudices, the more we can give attention to the context in which we are doing that seeing" (82). It is imperative when working with people that we apply this concept to the individuals to whom we are providing services and mentoring. If we do so, we are then able to embrace and practice flexibility.

Working with incarcerated people in a system that is not designed to be humane can be done. We can act in a humane manner to those who are incarcerated. Beyond the basics of humanity, love—yes, love—can be demonstrated. One of the chaplains at CCCF, Chaplain Emily Brault, is an incredible supporter of the Native spiritual services, as are the rest of the chaplains. Chaplain Brault shared these thoughts, which exemplify her service to all the women at CCCF:

> There's a song by Fred Small, who also happens to be a minister, asserting that "the only measure of your words and your deeds is the love you leave behind when you're done." It's a sweet and tender song, a song he sings to his kids as he tucks them in at night, a song that he wishes he had heard when he was coming up in the world. The bulk of the song is about being yourself, doing the things you want to do, loving the people you want to love, building your life according to love rather than societal prescriptions of The Shoulds. You know, who you should be, how you should live, what you should aspire to. And at the end of these admonishments of authentic living is this simple tagline that suggests that the substance of your life, the impact, the reckoning, perhaps, is not about where you live or how much you earn, how fancy your car is, how many exotic vacation spots you have under your belt. None of that. It's about love—and not just any love, but the kind of love that lingers about even after you've left the building, the kind of love that wakes people up in their

lives and sets up shop in their bones and reminds them that they aren't alone, that they matter, that they are loved. That's what counts. That's what's important. Not your bank account, but the quality of your love.

And then I think about the women I work with, the women and men in prison, who wear thick jackets of harm that's been done, to them and by them. Jackets that define them as Inmate, Con, Offender, Thief, Killer, Fighter, Player, Liar, Manipulator, and General Asshole. Jackets that fit some of them really well, show off their figure and make 'em strut down the hallway like they know someone. Jackets sometimes threadbare and worn at the elbows with ripped pockets that can tell stories of the places that this kid has been, and jackets that look fresh off the line with a stiff smell of new that hasn't been washed away yet.

And I know from experience that they, too, know how to love in ways that empower and support and impact people for the good. Some of them are amazing at it. Compassion, forgiveness, empathy—maybe not for themselves but when their friend is struggling, or their mom goes into surgery, or their kid has words to say to them that they might not want to hear, their love shows up like an embarrassing uncle at a family picnic. Might be a little rough around the edges but you know he's there, in all his blazing glory.

I hope that they, too, will be measured for the love they leave behind when they're done. They can never undo the harm that's been done, that's for sure. None of us can do that. But we can all move forward with greater awareness, greater appreciation for the impact that we have in the lives of other people, for the impact that we can have if we put our hearts into it. We all have jackets hanging in our closets somewhere, or maybe in the attic, or maybe in the storage shed we rent on the other side of town. Wherever. My point is, that jacket is never the last word. Or it doesn't have to be, anyway. It can be love, if you let it.

The idea of showing love to an inmate may seem implausible to some people. However, doing so is at the center of validation, of hope, of healing, and authentic humanity. In order to exhibit that love we need to suspend those beliefs ingrained by the Western world of who "deserves" to be treated humanely.

Peat (2008) advances the component of creative suspension in gentle action theory which he describes as "related to other approaches and techniques whereby unexamined assumptions and rigidities are brought into conscious awareness" (88). He proposes that "something new and more flexible could be reborn out of the breakdown of fixed patterns in an organization, policy group, or individual" (89). This is a difficult task, as the natural reaction in some cultures is often to act now to take care of a problem or get something done. Traditional Native communities practiced creative suspension when addressing societal issues. There were councils with chiefs and their group members, Elders, spirit leaders, and tribal members. The issue was discussed, pondered, and various courses of action were considered. Decisions were not made in haste, and all voices were heard. Peat (2008) states, "This new understanding would be the basis for a novel sort of action, one that harmonizes with nature and society" (92). Creative suspension is a healthy, respectful, and validating way to provide services and mentoring to Native women who are in prison or who have experienced incarceration. It provides a broader and deeper understanding of the needs and issues for each woman, and the ability to support them in finding creative ways for the women to react and address those needs and issues.

Another aspect of creative suspension is a deeper understanding of the "right" time to move into action. Peat shares an experience he had working with Native American Elders and Western scientists where they were to assemble for a pipe ceremony next to a lake on a given morning. The scientists waited a couple of hours for the Elders to arrive. When questioned on why they were late, the Elders replied, "The time was not right. We can only do this ceremony when the time is right" (Peat 2008, 99). Peat recounts that this was something he experienced many times from Native Americans. He understood that "time has a certain quality and that one should pause and suspend action until 'the time is right'" (99). For service providers and mentors to Native American women, the ability to wait and to know when the time is right is a helpful and needed skill to have and to model.

As discussed in chapter 5, examining and applying Peat's (2008) gentle action theory to the issue of Native American women's incarceration involves creating a different and more dynamic way that allows for both natural creativity and tacit knowledge. By investigating the systems of incarceration in a manner that is not conventional in its approach, activities can be generated that are creative, gentle, and highly intelligent. These activities therefore differ profoundly from conventional approaches that tend to be rigid, are externally directed, and only take a limited amount of information.

A Native American cultural norm is a respect for the tacit. In meetings involving members who are predominantly from Western culture, a noticeable aspect is their need to put forth their knowledge and experience; this is the way they look for approval. I notice this especially during the introduction time, and I have termed it the "Needy Opener." I usually just say my name and my tribal affiliation unless required to do more, and then I keep it succinct. We will have opportunities to get to know more about one another, at least what we are willing to show and share. Peat states, "Gentle action acts in a sensitive way to guide and refocus the energies and dynamics of the system in question" (2008, 141). He adds, "Gentle action and creative suspension are based on a general attitude towards rethinking the world, of not taking anything for granted, and being able to look in fresh ways" (142). Peat proposes that "gentle action goes beyond mere restructuring . . . to the invitation to each one of us to take responsibility for the creation of a new society" (144).

Working with and mentoring Native women who are incarcerated or who have experienced incarceration utilizing gentle action brings personal responsibility, empowerment, and validation of the skills and experiences of the women. It is not a method where the women are told what to do, when to do it, and how to do it. Clearly, that type of thinking and intervention has failed on a personal and systematic level.

As discussed earlier, at the beginning of our time together I had inquired of the women: How will you make sure that you don't reoffend? None of the women had a clear answer to that question. As we moved through the workshop, we discussed issues and provided information on topics ranging from their childhood, relationships, and parenting. We discussed historical trauma, fetal alcohol syndrome, and domestic violence. As trust and relationship were established with me and with one another, we discussed their criminality; an essential subject that cannot be ignored.

Incarceration and criminality have become ingrained in the Native experience. It has become accepted and often becomes a badge of honor. I recall being at a family gathering while home on my reservation and hearing my great-nephews discussing their experiences at a Montana juvenile facility. While there they saw some wooden storage boxes. Engraved on those boxes were the names of their fathers and uncles, and they too carved their names onto the boxes and joked about their own sons perhaps seeing those boxes one day. My heart was sick. While I was glad that they felt acceptance in their family and within the tribal community, I knew that I wanted that narrative to change to one of not expecting their sons to experience incarceration.

Another societal ill within the Native culture is the excusing and protecting of criminal behavior and family members. Many of us, myself included, come from a family who distrusts and even hates law enforcement. My mother is such an example. She hated it when one of her sons was taken away. I learned to fear law enforcement. I can clearly remember the day that most of us children were taken away from our parents. There was a line of sheriff vehicles to pick us all up. I was terrified and acutely aware that my siblings and I were being separated. I cried and cried for them.

There are a number of family stories about my mother, my brothers, and law enforcement. One such story involves my mother and a couple of my brothers. A sheriff was looking for one of my brothers, who had an outstanding warrant. He pulled up near my mother's trailer and with his bullhorn called out, "Joe, Joe Moreno, are you in there?" My brother Joe answered, "Joe's not here!" The sheriff asked, "Who are you?" My brother Joe answered, "I'm Vince." The sheriff went away. When hearing this story my family laughs and laughs. My mother who was there loved that story. She always had a scanner on, and she was determined to protect her boys if at all possible and had no qualms about aiding and abetting them. These are not unusual occurrences in Native families. I have heard of people flying their loved one out of state to protect them from answering to a violent crime they have committed.

Excuse-making is another societal reaction to one's own criminality or the criminality of a friend or family member. They were just in the wrong place at the wrong time, or they just drove the get-away car, and many other excuses instead of addressing, answering to, or admitting their crime. Addressing the acts that brought them to prison is a freeing action for the women. Some women did the crime they have been sentenced for, and other women are in because they are "taking the fall" for their significant other, but even those women were in some manner involved in the crime.

Gentle action also requires us to look at context, and that is imperative when listening to the recounting of crimes by the women. It is imperative because the majority of Native American women who are incarcerated are themselves victims of crime. American Indian and Alaska Native women have been victimized at a rate of 84.3 percent. They have experienced psychological aggression and physical violence by intimate partners. American Indian and Alaska Native women have experienced sexual violence at a rate of 56.1 percent and stalking at a rate of 48.8 percent (National Institute of Justice 2016). It is vital to comprehend that these statistics reflect adult women over the age of eighteen. As discussed earlier, many Native American women, and certainly the Native women who experience incarceration, have suffered crimes against them since they were young children. A 2018 report indicates: "The child abuse rate in the United States is highest among American Indian or Alaska Native victims with a rate of 15.2 cases per 1,000 children. It is most common among children between two to five years of age, with about 166,400 cases reported in 2017" (Statista 2022).

Unfortunately, for Native people it has become almost the norm to be sexually molested or assaulted as a child. It has been reported that on the average, American Indians ages twelve and older experience 5,900 sexual assaults per year (RAINN, n.d.). Child abuse statistics include the physical and the sexual, and while these numbers are shocking, they are never complete, as not every act is reported.

Gentle action theory does not advocate that we ignore the harm of the acts that the women have been involved in; rather it provides a process for the women, their families, and tribal communities as well as the larger society to understand the larger context of their experiences. By the end of our time together in the Healing the Sacred Hoop workshop, the women were able to process and discuss the criminality that had been part of their lives. Being able to do so provided a pathway for healing for them, their families, and their tribal communities. The women also came to terms with the reality that the process wouldn't be easy or rapid, and that the healing might be individualized. In some cases, family members who had been harmed had walked on, or their family as a whole was not healthy; the women also might not find acceptance in their tribal communities. They had to process their sadness and guilt about those realities, and it was painful. Working through all of these matters is painful and difficult, but gentle action theory offers an approach that integrates well with traditional ways of knowing and being.

Tony Ten Fingers (Oglala Lakota) reminds us that "mentoring another person is the forgotten dynamic which held humanity to embrace all the positive possibilities" (Ten Fingers 2014, 77).

These words resonate with me in my heart and spirit. Gentle action theory is about humanity and humaneness. Healing is about moving forward to find and embrace possibilities that one did not think were obtainable.

CHAPTER 8

Discoveries, Conclusion, and Future Research

It has been a long process of focusing on the issue of incarceration and Native American women, causing me to be more certain than ever about the issues and the need to continue the work. I contend that employing gentle action theory in Indian Country is an indispensable and exemplary method of addressing this societal issue and its ancillary effects.

It has been interesting examining a system that was created in a process that was never intended to exercise any form of gentle action, but rather is a system that began with a focus on physical pain and agony, with no acknowledgment of emotional pain. While contemporary systems within the United States and Canada have morphed into systems that have moved away from chain gangs, starvation, and physical violence, incarceration is nevertheless still about power, control, and punishment. The carceral system is still about controlling the body and is now even more about controlling the mind and spirit than the system was at its inception.

Examining traditional ways of justice practiced by Native American and First Nations people prior to first contact demonstrates considerable differences in how these societies administered justice as compared to the systems of colonialism. Native American and First Nations people did indeed have systems of justice. Native American and First Nations people had community members who committed crimes and who brought harm to their people and to their communities. It is imperative to recognize these realities, because far too often our history is romanticized by those outside our culture. Native people were not all holding hands, skipping, and singing an Indigenous version of the song "Kumbaya." There were wars, divisions, and controversies along with politics and family disputes. Tribal rivalry existed for territory, resources, and pride because they were human.

Gentle action theory has many elements that are modeled in traditional ways of knowing and being, and in the justice systems of our culture (Peat 2008). Fundamentally, gentle action theory is a model in which a problem is addressed within a community. As previously discussed, the experience of Native American people has too often been one in which those outside our communities have decided what problems we have, decreed what we should do about them, and determined what the end goals should be. The lack of understanding and accepting the subtleties of our culture, including kinship, family, and community systems, is not only unkind—it has been and still often is destructive and demeaning.

Gentle action theory, in contrast, offers an approach that is gentle, creative, and direct. It is also one of respect. It is respectful of people, culture, and place (Peat 2008). Native Americans are a people of place. Systems of kinship, creation stories, ceremonies, and culture are tied to place. Place is sacred as it is there that we find our beginnings, our ancestors, and the embodiment of our spiritual connections to the natural world. Respect is embodied in gentle action theory in a manner that blends well with traditional ways.

Gentle action theory is an approach of good motives. Basing action on what the community recognizes as a problem and the ways the community desires to seek the solution, the process has the potential to be one in which the community is satisfied with the end result (Peat 2008). Traditional ways of knowing and being are grounded in motives that seek what is the best for the community and individual members.

Gentle action theory is one of flexibility, creativity, and sensitivity (Peat 2008). Traditional ways of justice are flexible. There are no prescribed punishments for a crime. Rather, the perpetrator, the families of the perpetrator and the person who was harmed, and the Elders and tribal leaders weigh in on what remedy is most appropriate. Creativity comes into play when determining the remedy. If it is a property crime, some sort of compensation must be made. If the circle deems it appropriate that a lesson of character is needed, reparation can also include the perpetrator doing some form of community service or spending time with Elders to benefit from their wisdom. The Cree way is not one of shaming a person. My grandfather George Denny shared with me that if a child or young person does a task incorrectly, their Elder utters no words of recrimination, but rather takes the child or young person's hands in theirs and shows how to do the task correctly. The Cree understand that the heart and spirit of a person can be damaged by words or actions that are unkind, which then can lead to future problems for the person.

Gentle action theory is one that seeks harmony (Peat 2008). As discussed, traditional ways of knowing and being seek harmony in all aspects of culture and community. Any solution sought in traditional justice has at its center the restoration of relationship between the perpetrator, the person harmed, their families, and the community.

Gentle action theory is one of relationship and trust (Peat 2008). At the core of traditional ways of knowing and being are the tenets of relationship and trust. Too often those from outside our culture do not respect the time needed to build trust and relationships. We do not believe in or trust "instant" relationships. Rather, time needs to be taken to get to know each other, and through that process it is possible but not promised that relationship can be built. Center to any establishment of relationship is proven trustworthiness.

Gentle action theory in its practical applications is transformative. Addressing an issue, generating agreeable solutions, and implementing those solutions transforms the community and each individual involved in the process (Peat 2008). Traditional ways of knowing and being function in the same manner.

I have reflected on the tenets of gentle action theory and traditional ways of knowing from a Native American perspective, but I recognize that I have done so through my cultural lens as a Chippewa Cree tribal member whose familial connections are predominantly Cree. I am not a spokesperson for all Native American and First Nations people. Nevertheless,

I can ethically voice that there are norms across our tribal cultures that fit well with gentle action theory.

As I have done my research it has been a gift to learn more about my own people, culture, and history. What has become clear to me is that gentle action theory is not something new to Native American or First Nations people. Rather, it is a return to traditional ways of knowing and being. Gentle action theory is about the approach, which is sensitive, inclusive, and respectful; all of which are included in a traditional paradigm for our people.

When examining the needs of Native American women experiencing incarceration with a view to offering healing services, I found that gentle action theory was not only an appropriate but a necessary model. Working with the women in the Healing the Sacred Hoop workshop, I used gentle action theory from its inception to completion a year later. It was an amazing experience for the women, the presenters, and me. Trust was built and relationships were deepened among all of us involved. I have gone on to mentor five of the twelve women, continuing to apply the theory as I have mentored them. The trust and relationship along with the authenticity that gentle action theory propagates has validated my conjectures for its practical application.

INDIAN COUNTRY AND FUTURE WORK

Abril (2007), like Red Lodge, also found that Native American women in prisons are undercounted. There is much good work being done in Indian Country and, as part of an Indigenous research paradigm, I look forward to adding to the body of work being done. It would be impossible for me to know about and list all the available programs, but here are a few that I am able to highlight.

Healing Lodges of Canada: There are a number of Healing Lodges for men. In 1995 the first for women was opened and is called Okimaw Ohci, which means "thunder hills" in Cree. The buildings are circular, with the central building being the spiritual lodge. It is here that teachings, ceremonies, and workshops with Elders take place. There are both single and family residential units; some offenders may have their children stay with them. The programs offered help the women to create plans that meet their emotional, physical, and spiritual needs. "The vision that was instilled at Okimaw Ohci Healing Lodge was developed by the Elders who guided the planning and practices at the facilities with five principles: empowerment, meaningful and responsible choices, respect and dignity, supportive environment and shared responsibility" (Advantage 2016).

Port Gamble S'Klallam Re-Entry Program: The program's mission is to remove barriers to employment for tribal members who have a criminal history while providing services to help them find and retain employment. The program uses a strengths-based approach. Program participants can also be referred for additional services such as Moral Recognition Therapy, along with treatment for chemical dependency and mental health services, support groups, or educational classes. There is a cultural coach on staff. Classes are offered on traditional ways, spiritual teachings, and family and community values. Program participants learn how to design and make drums and drumsticks. They can learn traditional beading techniques. They also can learn how to harvest cedar and gather and prepare traditional foods and plants for ceremonies (Tribal Access to Justice Innovation, n.d.).

Muscogee (Creek) Nation Reintegration Program: The program's mission is to "protect the public by offering quality re-entry services to Mvskoke Citizens and re-invest positive citizens back into their communities" (Tribal Access to Justice Innovation 2022). They believe that "every Citizen, even an ex-prisoner, is important," that "everybody is capable of change," and that "investments in our people are investments in the Nation's strength and sovereignty." The program

> encourages a high degree of understanding, cooperation, efficiency, accountability and unity through an application of offender wrap-around re-entry practices with cultural focus.
>
> provides information affecting re-entry and transition to tribal, state, federal, and community stakeholders, [and they] cultivate an awareness for the need of re-entry services.
>
> promotes positive re-entry conditions that shall support the practice of individual responsibility with the Muscogee (Creek) Nation Community.

fosters a celebration of success for citizens and their contribution toward a renewal of family and spiritual growth, thereby, celebrating their accomplishments, and

empowers clients to facilitate their tradition through an environment of positive change.

RESTORATIVE JUSTICE

Many tribes utilize restorative justice in their courts and as part of an ongoing process to reclaim traditional ways. The Navajo Nation has long been making great strides in decolonizing their legal procedures and returning to the traditional ways through the Navajo peacekeeping process. I am fortunate to know the Honorable Robert Yazzie, the chief justice emeritus of the Navajo Nation Supreme Court. I hosted a Peace-making Symposium at Lewis and Clark Law School with Justice Yazzie as the keynote speaker. In an interview with the International Institute for Restorative Practices, Justice Yazzie described the life way as the teachings of the *Diyin Dine'é*, the Holy People.

Asked to define the Holy People, Yazzie said, "We don't have a word for religion. We don't have a word for God. *Diyin Dine'é* means the Holy People who were responsible for the creation of the world. They are present everywhere: in the fire, in the water, in the air that we breathe, the things that grow."

Asked what is meant by Navajo common law, Yazzie commented, "Of course that's the English term," then explained, "There's a word that covers everything: *beehaz-aanii*: the laws or the principles or the teachings that were given to the five-finger people by the Holy People." Some of those, he said, are used in prayers and ceremonies, "and some of those are so sacred that they can't be shared, but others—*beehaz-aanii*—are used to teach the life way."

"For example," said Yazzie, "Let's say you and I got into a squabble, and you hit me over the head. In the Western world, you would be called a defendant in a criminal proceeding and would create a bad name for yourself. The Western law way is to punish you, so that you don't repeat the behavior. But the Navajo way is to focus on the individual. You separate the action from the person. The Holy People say that the human being is a creation of the Holy People, and we have no part, we cannot destroy the human being or change it to something else. It's not within our authority to do that. In fact, what you must do is respect yourself, because you are the creation of the Holy People. If you and I were to squabble and I sued you for criminal liability, civil liability, the *Diyin Dine'é* would say you should be respected. What is not respected is what you did."

The Navajo peacemaking process helps an offender realize that what he or she has done is incorrect. The process brings the offender and the victim together to talk to each other. "The first order of business the relatives would do in the peacemaking process is to get to the bottom of a problem," he said. "In court, I would sue you for battery and the state would say we have to prove all the elements of a crime and use the rules or the law to prove that you are guilty. The Holy People say that's beside the point. What matters here is: why did this act happen in the first place? There's a reason why the harm has occurred. Let's deal with that. Maybe we have a history of problems between the two of us. If we can get to the bottom of a problem, all the other stuff will fall into place. The damage can be acknowledged by you, and I can go away happy from the process, knowing that you say that you're not going to do it again."

The peacemaking process is related to the concept of *k'e*, or respect, said Yazzie, adding, "*K'e* means to restore my dignity, to restore my worthiness." Through the peacemaking process, an offender can come to feel better, said Yazzie, especially when the person can say, "'I'm responsible, I'm accountable.' That does a lot to the spirit, the mind and the body of those who participate in the process," he said.

Not only are the victim and the offender involved in the process, like in Western law, said Yazzie, "but the relatives would also feel relief, and those who are also interested in the process would feel the same way. So in the end, there's healing at different levels."

Peacemaking can work with any problem, said Yazzie. In the Western way, he said, "you divide up things, and you say that certain types of cases should go to peacemaking. That's what I'm hearing today. There's a distrust, since the Western legal system has control over everything. It doesn't leave room for anything. The judges are in there; the lawyers are in there. So the type of process we work with, we close the door on everybody and let the parties feel that they own the problem, let them choose who they want to facilitate the process." (Mirsky 2004).

Justice Yazzie in his description of the Navajo peacemaking process illustrates the juxtaposition between traditional ways and gentle action theory. Central to the concept is that it is a process that comes from within a community to address societal issues of that community. In addition, the Navajo peacemaking process calls for all the stakeholders and its goals are respect, trust, relationship, and balance.

Judge Abby Abinanti of the Yurok Tribal Court is another person whom I am fortunate to know. At Lewis and Clark Law School, I hosted a screening of the film *Tribal Justice*, with panel discussion led by Judge Abinanti. In an interview with Rebecca Clarren in the *Nation*, Judge Abinanti explains, "I'm looking at: How did we resolve things before our cultural interruption, when invasion occurred? We were village people, and we sat around and had discussions. My purpose is to help you think up how to make it right if you made a mistake. . . . For me, jail is banishment. It's the last resort" (Clarren 2017).

In another interview for the Open California Oral History Project, Judge Abinanti describes the Yurok Wellness Court:

The Wellness Court is really . . . a collaborative court and many of our people have as a result of the invasion and the aftermath . . . picked up some really bad habits and we have to look at those habits ourselves, and go, "What are we going to do? How am I going to get past this bad habit, can I get past this bad habit? Can I walk back down the road that I came to, and make a different choice?" And that's what the Wellness Court is about. And we were talking this morning with some of the wellness staff, when you see a pattern of people starting to have trouble after five or six years, when they've been in a good place for five or six years and we've got a couple, two or three that are doing that now, I want to turn our attention back to those people and go, "Maybe we didn't give them enough support for long enough and maybe we need to stay in their lives longer. And just because they're still not on the docket this is the list of people I need you to go see." Do they need to come back in? Do they need to be back in wellness? Because I know that they're doing things now that they don't approve of themselves. This is not how they want it to be. (Frampton 2019)

Judge Abinanti describes key aspects of gentle action theory and traditional ways, highlighting an allowance for people making mistakes, and a process where the court, family and community, and the offender all recognize that recidivism occurs. The focus becomes an effort to determine what offenders need to be well and to address wrongs they have committed, rather than ramping up punishment of the perpetrator. She stresses the collaborative process that is a key tenet of gentle action theory.

These programs are a very small representation of programs being offered in Indian Country addressing incarceration and reentry. It is my goal to offer workshops on gentle action theory both to existing programs and to tribes and Native organizations desiring to offer programs.

Small steps are good steps when it comes to the prison industrial complex. Recently the Washington State Department of Corrections announced that Washington prison inmates will no longer be called "offenders." Instead, staff will use terms like "individual," and staff are encouraged to address inmates by name. The State of Washington joins the State of Oregon Department of Corrections in changing what prisoners are called. Oregon recently began using the term "adults in custody" (Jenkins 2016). While these changes are a good replacement for the terms "inmate" and "prisoner," our sisters and brothers are still criminals in the minds of society, and they are still incarcerated. I appreciate the words of Gabe Galanda, chairman of the nonprofit Huy, who said, "We'll stick with 'brothers' and 'sisters' when referring to our people behind bars" (Facebook post, November 4, 2016). A 2012 front-page story in *Willamette Week*, in Portland, Oregon, was titled "Jail Birds, the Fastest-Growing Group of Inmates in Oregon Women: A Look Inside Coffee Creek" and included a full-page color photo of women inmates. Following news stories after 2012, the Department of Corrections has begun using "adults in custody" when interviewed.

The Vera Institute of Justice announced on its website: "Mayors, Chamber of Commerce leaders, public school teachers, physicians, prosecutors, faith leaders, and other community members will visit prisons and jails in

17 geographically and politically diverse states, from Nebraska and Michigan, to New Jersey, North Carolina, and Ohio as part of National Prison Visiting Week" (Vera, n.d.). It is part of an effort to increase the understanding of incarceration and its conditions. Additionally, its goal is to advance transparency of the operation of facilities while fostering public engagement around criminal justice reform. Vera's Reimagining Prison initiative objective is to "produce a vision for a system of incarceration that is significantly smaller, rooted in human dignity, effective for public and facility safety, and committed to helping people succeed upon release." I appreciate their desire to break down the barriers between prisons and the larger society. It coalesces well with the efforts of myself and many others working on behalf of Native Americans in prison to make the invisible visible.

GENERAL PUBLIC

It is difficult for the general public to understand and to be willing to learn about reentry, because of both an attitude bias and the unavailability of in-depth training. Reinventing Reentry, an Arizona nonprofit, actively promotes education to the community and former inmates.

The organization Reinventing Reentry was founded by Sue Ellen Allen. Allen is a former inmate at the Arizona State Prison who is also a graduate of the University of Texas, an educator, a community leader, and an activist. She recognized that large-scale change would only happen when the general public became informed about the current prison system. Allen found her life's purpose from serving time in prison. The organization offers a reentry simulation that is an interactive event held over two hours. Attendees have the opportunity to experience the challenges inmates face upon release from prison.

According to their website, "The Reentry Simulation illustrates the enormous challenges faced by those returning from incarceration. The simulation raises awareness, outrage and empathy about the reentry process and makes obvious for any audience the need for more creative solutions and compassion for those impacted" (Reinventing Reentry 2020). These desired goals of creative solutions and compassion parallel with traditional ways and gentle action theory. The Reentry Simulation works to answer the following questions:

Who is coming out of prison and what's the first month like for them?

Why do some people go back to prison after their release?

What can be done to increase the likelihood of success for people reentering their communities?

I am hoping either to hold a Reentry Simulation at my university or to attend one as a participant. Due to the founder and presenter being ill, I have not yet been able to attend a workshop. As stated earlier, part of my work is to "make the invisible visible," applying gentle action theory as the method, and the model and mission of the organization seems germane.

FELONS MAKING A DIFFERENCE

Out in the world of the general public there is a misconception that inmates are either in chain gangs or using the government's money to earn college degrees, or that they are sitting around doing nothing or starting fights out in the "yard." There is no real understanding or even interest in the cultural traditions that are carried out behind bars.

Frank Hopper, writing for *Last Real Indians*, shares a story about the Tribal Sons Native American Inmate Spirituality Circle at the Washington Corrections Center in Shelton, Washington:

> Jay Powell, a member of the Squaxin Island Tribe who [was and who still might be] incarcerated at Washington Corrections Center, knitted a cap and a scarf for an inmate he'd just met. The man was about to be released in the dead of winter, homeless, and Powell was worried he might freeze to death.
>
> Powell received permission from staff to use a small loom to knit the items and gave them to the man. When he was released back out onto the cold streets, at least the man's head and neck were warm courtesy of Powell.
>
> Word got around and a few other inmates began asking Powell about the caps and scarves. They didn't want Powell to make them some. They wanted to learn how to do it themselves, to make things and give them to needy people.
>
> [The brothers have gone on to do other projects, including making] 40 decorated wooden boxes filled with toys and gifts they made themselves. They donated them to children of the Squaxin Island Tribe who are currently in foster care.

Christmas season, 2018, members of the Squaxin Island Tribe, including Tribal Chairman Arnold Cooper, received the gifts for the tribe's foster children during a visit to the prison. During that visit, traditional honoring, singing, and gift giving were carried out, which is the center of the Native Northwest coastal tradition of potlatch, a ceremony of feasting and the exchange of gifts. Holding the ceremony with tribal leadership and tribal members was deeply meaningful for the Native brothers.

Powell and other inmates belong to the Tribal Sons Native American Inmate Spirituality Circle at the prison. The program is for Native inmates of any tribe. They meet twice a week with the meetings led by Native sponsors from nearby communities. The Native brothers learn and share cultural traditions, such as drumming, singing, storytelling, and making sacred regalia. They are able to hold a sweat lodge twice a month. Powell pronounced how giving has acted as a powerful medicine for the brothers. "It reaches a deeper level than just giving back. It really touches these brothers' souls in here and helps them. For a lot of the bros, this is the first time they've ever been a part of something like this" (Hopper 2020).

The efforts of the Tribal Sons combined with the Native American liaison, the nonprofit Native American Reentry Services, and the local tribal communities demonstrate the foundations of gentle action theory in what we Native people term "a good way." Addressing and meeting the needs of the brothers to receive healing, to make amends, and to access culture and tribal connection are done from within the Native society. Respect and trust are formed, as are relationships. In addition, being able to do those things within larger oppressive and punitive systems and society as a whole is both necessary and remarkable.

FORMERLY INCARCERATED

Jonel Beauvais

Through my work in Indian Country I learned of the reentry work being done by the Seven Dancers Coalition based in Akwesasne, New York, which is home to the Mohawks of Akwesasne (Seven Dancers Coalition 2019). I had the privilege of presenting at a national conference where Jonel Beauvais (Kaianahawis [she's carrying the footprints of the Creator]–Wolf Clan–Mohawk) from Akwesasne was speaking on "The Power to Heal: Incarceration and the Indigenous Experience" and the work of the Seven Dancers Coalition. Upon my return home I began researching the site and wanted to learn more about Jonel. After doing some research, I reached out to Jonel, who graciously shared information about her work with the Seven Dancers Coalition and her personal story with me:

The site itself (Seven Dancers Coalition) is intended to help support non-violent offenders to be released early due to the inhuman treatment towards the people incarcerated, along with a hotline for those inside needing help. Having went to prison myself I am well aware of the already abusive environment inside from prison staff and witnessed the justification of abuse towards people just because they have power to do so. They believe they have the right to treat people less than human because they are in prison and that somehow that is supposed to make things "right" or "fair." Witnessing daily the abuse of power the staff used against us made me angry! I wanted people to learn the truth! I wanted them to be held accountable for what they did to me and others. All I could do after coming home was tell my story, I have nothing to gain than to stay true to the fact I was at least honoring the truth instead of wallowing in the injustices in the name of justice. I lived, ate, walked, talked, slept beside people who were responsible for taking a life. They became my friends and family I needed while I was in there. Most of them were doing a minimum of twenty-five to life. I heard their stories, seen pictures of their kids, and I was able to build relationships that made me a better person. I loved those women and will hold them in my heart always. This is where I learned the depths of compassion. I learned that no one is ever free from the choices they make, inside prison or not. I had to do a lot of personal work on myself and still do in order to bring my best to those that cause harm and those that receive it, sometimes they are the same person. I learned using violence to fight violence is not productive for anyone and either way more pain is caused. I also got to learn more about restorative justice and transformational justice. I found out that we have only relied on punishment and not left enough room for change and growth. We have all become the prosecutors and judges, not enough good defense. But this isn't about picking sides this is about common ground, it is about the love people carry for their family, and no one should take that away from them, one is not more valuable than the other. There are just better ways for us to hold space for everyone affected by violence. There are lots of sources that create it but mostly pain and lack of love. [Recognizing the sources helps us identify] the remedy to causing harm to ourselves and others. I take full responsibility for any unintentional harm I may have caused anyone yesterday. I do not know all the details around a lot of situations. I removed it because I don't believe in causing harm to address harm. I do my best to work with care and understanding and if I have not done that it is ok to tell me. This work is very difficult and there are many in our community who help in their own way to try and bring healing into it. That's why we are here, so no one in the community has to suffer alone, nobody suffers more than children do. But we have witnessed healing, felt it and that is how we know it is possible, but the intent was to bring support to families and individuals who usually get very little of that. We all make choices and have to learn to live with them. I am trying to be the kind of community I want to live in, a healthier, safer one. Nia:wen (Thank you) and sending my love to you! (Beauvais 2019)

After receiving this message from Jonel, I was privileged to speak with her on the telephone. I asked her to tell me about her decision to work in reentry. She told me:

Prison taught me that it is easy to discard people and throw them away. I didn't want that treatment for our people; they had been through enough of that! I didn't want that for another child who has to grieve a living parent because the system didn't work to keep them together. I was hoping things had changed, but I was merely experiencing the generational trauma of systematic oppression and the attempt to distinguish my identity and personal power. I had won my appeal and realized there was no words like reentry in the resources for our community. There was nothing! Today there is still not much besides us here at Seven Dancers Coalition. Thankfully our director Amie heard our stories and believed in us to initiate ceremony and encourage family and community discussion around what was happening to our families, and the damaged caused by not having certain supports in place to generate better cycles of recovery and healing. I have prayed many times to be guided, to do the right thing in the midst of anger and loss. Prayed to heal and not become more of who I wasn't, but to do something that made the time I lost into something so special it would leave the message to my own children that you don't ever let someone tell you who you are and what you're made of!! That everything about them came from a woman who chose her children, her commitment to her prayer, and the spirit of the people she learned to love through her own mother. That's how powerful we really are. That's the spirit of an Indigenous woman!

I asked her to describe the "Walking Home" of a tribal member who is exiting incarceration and returning to community:

The "welcoming home the spirit" ceremony is an opportunity for the individual to be "cleaned off" spiritually, so they don't have to carry the violence from the institution back into their families and the community. It is also intended for the family to have a safe and supported time to acknowledge the journey they have been through, and show them that there are others in the community willing to help their relative transition and work through some of the anxiety being institutionalized can cause. We will do an opening address, to acknowledge creation for all of the gifts of life that sustain us. We then move forward with the words of encouragement from everyone in attendance, including invited community members from law enforcement and traditional leadership. Anyone is able to attend if they wish to. We always save the individual for last so they may also express themselves as well. From there we will share a meal provided by the family or community program. Then get ready to enter the sweat lodge, where many more prayers and songs will be shared. After the sweat everyone is feeling the medicine of the ceremony, which is a really good feeling of peace and love. We will thank everyone for coming and all help to clean up! (Beauvais 2020)

Jonel shared that their services are offered in the traditional way of their people. They consult with cultural leaders and look to their teachings often, in order to find the best way to address their healing. They always start the ceremony with gratitude and natural medicines such as sweet grass and sage. Certain songs are shared. Traditional instruments such as feather fans and a pipe are used in the ceremony.

I was drawn by the purpose and carrying out of the "Walking Home" ceremony. Both the ceremony and the manner in which it is conducted interface well with gentle action theory. I wish that all tribes and Native groups had and practiced a "Walking Home" ceremony. Jonel and I hope to see each other at a conference or two next year and continue to stay in touch.

Tosha Big Eagle

A friend told me of an article she had read about the formerly incarcerated Native woman Tosha Big Eagle, who is attending college near me, and my friend wanted me to read her story. Tosha is at Clark College in Vancouver, Washington, working toward an associate's degree in addiction counseling, and plans to transfer to Washington State University's campus in Vancouver to earn a bachelor's degree in human development. She is a member of the Re-Entry Club at the college. Miguel Viveros (2020) wrote about her in Clark College's student news publication. I was intrigued reading Tosha's story of incarceration, her return to college, her experience as a student who has been incarcerated, and the Re-Entry Club. I reached out to her and was able to schedule a telephone interview with her.

Tosha has found the Re-Entry Club an accepting place and as a core member is determined that the culture of the club be inclusive and supportive. She cited her experience while in prison and her involvement in Native groups as difficult. She talked about acts of lateral oppression and divisiveness that occur often. These acts include leaders who create schisms within the group by deciding who is "Indian enough" to be included in the group. The culture of these groups tends to be chaotic, and leaders exert power and control. I have certainly witnessed this type of leadership, and it does not promote healing.

Tosha took these experiences to heart and became a leader of an informal group called "Women's Village." The group is composed of women who have all been incarcerated and are now back in community. The women come from many different backgrounds and ethnicities. One of their core services is doing peer mentoring. Tosha emphasized that the group's model is one of acceptance, respect, and support. It is about helping members find community as they reenter the larger community. Tosha and I discussed gentle action theory and traditional ways and found that many of the tenets of those systems meld well with the culture they are building in the Women's Village group. I promised that I would gift her F. David Peat's book and we will stay in touch (Big Eagle 2020).

CONTEMPORARY TIMES AND LUANA ROSS
(CONFEDERATED SALISH AND KOOTENAI TRIBES)

At the beginning of my PhD program, I knew I wanted to concentrate on the societal issue of the incarceration of Native American women. My first research query produced only one book and one author writing on the subject: Dr. Luana Ross. Of course, I wanted to meet her, speak with her, and if it all possible have her on my dissertation committee. Indian Country is both large and small, with a web of interconnectedness. I knew that someone I knew and probably many people had to know Luana. The first person I reached out to was my friend Bob Miller (Eastern Shawnee), who at that time was still teaching at Lewis and Clark Law School. Of course, Bob knew her and agreed to introduce me to Luana "virtually."

I am fortunate to have gotten to know Luana, to have had her counsel, and to have become her friend. In the fall of 2018 I was invited by Luana to be a panelist at the Alexander Blewett III School of Law's "Indigenous Feminisms Symposium: Bad Indians, Stolen Children, and Journeys Home," in Missoula, Montana. Spending time with Luana in person was amazing and further energized me in my effort to publish my work. Recently Luana graciously agreed to let me interview her. I wanted to know her thoughts some twenty plus years after publishing her book, *Inventing the Savage: The Social Construction of Native American Criminality* (1998). Here is a short transcript of our interview:

What drew you to writing your book, Inventing the Savage: The Social Construction of Native American Criminality?

LUANA: I was doing my PhD research and wanted to make a difference in the lives of Native women being incarcerated. I wanted to trigger policy changes. I had relatives in prison as well as those who had been in prison and then returned home. I wanted to give Native women in prison a voice.

Here we are in the year 2020, have you seen improvements in the criminal justice system in terms of Native American women's experiences of incarceration?
LUANA: No! There have been tiny changes. Band-Aids have been applied. There have been no systematic changes!

What are some of the things that are concerning to you?
LUANA: Poor healthcare within the prison system. Even prior to the current situation of COVID-19, there have never been enough hospital beds or healthcare for women prisoners. Racism is overt and rampant.

In discussing reentry for Native American women, what is something you are aware of?
LUANA: Tribes are not doing enough! We need to be serving our people with ethical programs and support. Tribal and family politics get in the way of developing programs and making decisions about individuals versus the traditional way of serving all people. In addition, tribal and family feuds hamper traditional restorative justice. The case of a Northern Cheyenne comes to mind: she gave testimony against those who had committed a crime and was then banished by her own people for doing so. She was in a sense left without a country for choosing to do the right thing.

For those of us advocating for Native American women experiencing incarceration, what would you like to see us doing?
LUANA: Carma, you are doing it all! Please continue with the work!
(At this point, I was crying because Luana's friendship, wisdom, and support mean so much to me as Native woman, a scholar, and an activist.)

FUTURE RESEARCH

A number of areas of needed future research have emerged. Research can be done with both qualitative and quantitative methods. However, doing research with Native women using quantitative methods will prove more difficult, as it is difficult to track women once they leave prison and are off probation unless they are part of a program or an ongoing relationship is developed. Native researchers employing an Indigenous research paradigm to address the needs of Native American women inmates can conduct studies with dignity, respect, cultural connection, and spirituality while developing a relationship with the participants. There is a plethora of theories that can be employed and are applicable to many fields of study, including sociology, psychology, restorative justice, ethnography, narrative, social work, or any of the other research approaches. It is up to the researchers to find their passion for the research, and the theory and method will follow; and as Kovach (2009) asserts, for the Indigenous researcher, Indigenous theory and practice is a valid and practical option.

There is no doubt that future research is needed, and research that focuses on Native American women incarcerated in the United States is essential if we are to address the issue of incarceration that so deeply affects our people. Abril's study on identity data from Native American women incarcerated at the Ohio Reformatory for women found that pride in one's Indian identity was important to the women as a connection to their heritage, culture, and spiritual activities and aided in their healing from the effects of violence in their lives (Abril 2007). She calls for further research not solely as a means of obtaining a more accurate accounting of Native American women prisoners but also for researchers, stakeholders, and reformers to see to the well-being of Native American women prisoners in better ways.

Identity as a Native American is a fundamental component in the healing process. The concept of identity was threaded throughout the Healing the Sacred Hoop workshop. The women explored and developed a greater sense of the way they thought of themselves, who their people are, and their place in the world. Cordova (1994) writes on identity and the Native American experience in a piece called *Who We Are: An Exploration of Identity*. The whole piece is meaningful, but as it is quite extended, sections shared here are some that correlate with the discussions in the workshop.

Columbus thought he was in paradise
The people, he said
For he thought they were people—are kind and generous
and share all that they have.
And then
    they become
    savages
    cannibals
    devil worshippers
    heathens
    Indians
but
they had souls
said the Pope
and if they had souls
they could be converted
and if they could be converted
—from heathen to Christian—
they could be used as beasts of burden . . .
to build edifices
for the glory of god
and civilization
a brick
at a time
A couple of generations
later
"Indians"—for that is
what we became to be called—
were seen as
Noble Savages
We graced their coins and imaginations,
Except of course—
where we still
outnumbered them
Out West . . .

And finally when the numbers
Had fallen
they, too
out west
became noble savages
For the purposes
Of missionaries
anthropologists
psychologists
ethnologists
painters
sculptors
and
Edward S. Curtis . . .
But we are not solitary . . .
We are part of the whole
The "I" is a unique combination
of the group
that brings the "I"
into existence
"I" am the sum
of the group
of its experiences
its knowledge
"I" became "I"
when I have learned
my place in the group
when I became aware
of the fact
that my actions
have consequences
on others
on the whole
only then
am "I" a person (Cordova 1994, 134–41)

While I have researched gentle action theory as an approach to address the issue of incarceration for Native American women prisoners while providing culturally specific programs of healing, gentle action theory can be applied to any societal issue by any community.

When Barbara (Klamath) and I chatted, I asked her if she recalled me sharing about gentle action theory at our preliminary meeting. She remembered my discussing my research but did not recall the details of the theory and asked me to refresh her memory. Once I had done so, Barbara remembered me talking about it and my sharing the guidelines for the workshop. She shared her reflections on our eighteen months together and her feelings about the application of the theory in the way I conducted the workshop.

Barbara shared that she felt that the experience was one of consistency, authenticity, and respect. She felt empowered to explore her feelings, her life experience, and her thoughts about life after prison. She did not feel as though she was being told what to do or what to feel. She felt welcomed and validated and felt the sisterhood was strengthened in a positive way. She felt it was a place where she could be herself and be open and honest about her feelings and her struggles. Barbara felt that trust and respect were built with her and the other members of the group and with me. She came with an immature sense of self. Throughout the process, she formed a matured sense of self, her place in the world and a dream of a life she could create when leaving prison. To me, there can be no greater example of how gentle action theory can be applied in working with Native American women who are incarcerated and who are seeking healing. I humbly close with a prayer that I shared with the women of the Healing the Sacred Hoop workshop as I give thanks to Creator and the Ancestors.

> O Great Spirit, whose Voice I hear in the Winds,
> Hear me—for I am small and weak:
> I need Your Strength and Wisdom.
> I seek Strength, O Great One, not to be superior to my Brothers—
> But to conquer my greatest enemy: Myself.
> I seek Wisdom: the Lessons You have hidden

In every Leaf and Rock so that I may learn
And carry these messages of Life and Hope to my People.
May my hands respect the many beautiful things You have made;
May my ears be sharp—to hear Your voice.
May I always walk in Your beauty;
And let my eyes behold the red and purple Sunset
So that when Life fades with the setting Sun,
My Spirit will come to You without shame.

(Chief Yellow Lark, Lakota, 1887)

REFERENCES

Aboriginal Education Directorate. 2014. "Smudging Protocol and Guidelines." http://www.edu.gov.mb.ca/aed/publications/pdf/smudging_guidelines.pdf.

Abril, Julie C. 2007. "Native American Indian Women: Implications for Prison Research." *Southwest Journal of Criminal Justice* 4 (2): 133–44. http://swacj.org/swjcj/archives/4.2/7%20abril.pdf.

ACLU (American Civil Liberties Union). 2015. *Locked in the Past: Montana's Jails in Crisis.* https://www.aclumontana.org/sites/default/files/field_documents/2015-aclu-jail-report.pdf.

———. 2017. "Words from Prison—Did You Know?" https://www.aclu.org/other/words-prison-did-you-know.

Advantage. 2016. "Okimaw Ohci Healing Lodge." https://advantagegrp.ca/case-studies/2017/12/7/okimaw-ohci-healing-lodge.

AJIC (Aboriginal Justice Implementation Commission). 2001. "Aboriginal Concepts of Justice." In *Report of the Aboriginal Justice Inquiry of Manitoba.* http://www.ajic.mb.ca/volumel/chapter2.html.

———. n.d. Home page. http://www.ajic.mb.ca/.

Alexander, Michelle. 2010. *Mass Incarceration in the Age of Colorblindness.* New York: New Press.

Allard, Patricia. 2002. *Life Sentences: Denying Welfare Benefits to Women Convicted of Drug Offenses.* February 2002. https://www.opensocietyfoundations.org/sites/default/files/03-18-03atriciaAllardReport.pdf.

American Indian Movement. 2022. "Effects of Termination." https://americanindianmovementehs.weebly.com/indian-termination-policy.html.

American Indian Relief Council. n.d. "History and Culture: Termination Policy 1953–1968." http://www.nrcprograms.org/site/PageServer?pagename=airc _hist_terminationpolicy.

American Psychiatric Association. 2010. "Mental Health Disparities: American Indian and Alaska Natives" (fact sheet). Last accessed October 15, 2015. http://www .integration.samhsa.gov/workforce/mental_health_disparities_american_indian _and_alaskan_natives.pdf (site discontinued).

Anishnawbe Mushkiki Community Health & Wellness Aboriginal Health Access Centre. 2022. "Traditional Teaching: Sweat Lodge." https://mushkiki.com/our -programs/sweat-lodge/.

Bailey, Everton, Jr. 2019. "Oregon Transgender Prisoner Must Have Transgender Cellmate or Be Housed Alone, Judge Says." *Oregonian*, May 31, 2019.

Baumann, Lisa. 2015. "State Unemployment Report Includes Reservation Data." *Great Falls Tribune*, June 19, 2015. http://www.greatfallstribune.com/story/news/2015 /06/19/state-unemployment-rate-report-includes-reservation-data/28994267/.

Beauvais, Jonel. 2019. Personal communication, November 4, 2019.

———. 2020. Telephone interview, January 23, 2020.

Bell, Jamaal. 2010. "Mass Incarceration: A Destroyer of People of Color and Their Communities." *Huffington Post*, May 17, 2010. http://www.huffingtonpost.com /jamaal-bell/mass-incarceration-a-dest_b_578854.html (site closed).

Benton, Ashley. 2019. "Trauma-Informed Education: Addressing School-to-Prison Pipeline." *Odyssey Online*, May 16, 2019. https://odyssey.antiochsb.edu/student -activism/trauma-informed-education-addressing-school-to-prison-pipeline/.

Beran, Stephanie. 2005. "Native Americans in Prison: The Struggle for Religious Freedom." *Nebraska Anthropologist* 20: 46–55. https://digitalcommons.unl.edu /cgi/viewcontent.cgi?article=1001&context=nebanthro.

Big Eagle, Tosha. 2020. Personal communication, December 17, 2020.

Brave Heart, Maria Yellow Horse. 1999. "*Oyate Ptayela*: Rebuilding the Lakota Nation through Addressing Historical Trauma among Lakota Parents." *Journal of Human Behavior in Social Environment* 2 (1–2): 109–26. http://dx.doi.org/10 .1300/j137v02n01_08.

———. 2000. "*Wakiksuyapi*: Carrying the Historical Trauma of the Lakota." *Tulane Studies in Social Welfare* 21–22: 245–66.

———. 2015. "Historical Trauma and Its Effect on Our Community." Lecture presented at Protecting Our Children, the 33rd annual National Indian Child Welfare Association Conference on Child Abuse and Neglect, Portland OR, April 20, 2015.

Brayboy, D. 2016. "Two Spirits, One Heart, Five Genders" (opinion). *Indian Country*, January 23, 2016. http://indiancountrytodaymedianetwork.com/2016/01/23 /two-spirits-one-heart-five-genders.

Buttenwieser, S. 2016. "Women's Incarceration: Frequent Starting Point Is Child-hood Abuse" (commentary). *Women's Media Center*, March 22, 2016. http://www.womensmediacenter.com/feature/entry/womens-incarceration-frequent-starting-point-is-childhood-abuse.

Canadian Senate Committee on Human Rights. 2017. "Life on the Inside: Human Rights in Canada's Prisons." June 1, 2017. https://sencanada.ca/en/sencaplus/news/life-on-the-inside-human-rights-in-canadas-prisons/.

Chavers, Dean. 2002. "The Lumbee Controversy." *Seminole Tribune*, July 5, 2002. Accessed May 15, 2021. http://search.proquest.com.libdata.lib.ua.edu/ethnicnewswatch/docview/362599353/bf9f1da209d34d25pq/9?accountid=14472.

Chief Yellow Lark. 1887. "Great Spirit Prayer." World Prayers. http://www.worldprayers.org/archive/prayers/invocations/oh_great_spirit_whose_voice.html.

Chippewa Cree Cultural Resources Preservation Department. 2014. "Our History." http://nei-yahw.com/historical.html.

Clarren, Rebecca. 2017. "Judge Abby Abinanti Is Fighting for Her Tribe—and for a Better Justice System." *Nation*, November 30, 2017. https://www.thenation.com/article/archive/judge-abby-abinanti-is-fighting-for-her-tribe-and-for-a-better-justice-system/.

Cordova, V. F. 1994. *Who We Are: An Exploration of Identity*. Fort Collins: Colorado State University.

Correctional Service Canada. 2019. "Indigenous Healing Lodges." September 5, 2019. https://www.csc-scc.gc.ca/aboriginal/002003-2000-en.shtml.

Cree Nation. 1993. *Mista Muskwa (Big Bear) Monument on the Poundmaker Cree Nation* (photo). July 16, 1993. https://treaty6education.lskysd.ca/bigbear.

Criminal Justice Degrees Guide. 2017. "A Day in the Life of a Prisoner." Accessed November 4, 2017. http://www.criminaljusticedegreesguide.com/features/a-day-in-the-life-of-a-prisoner.html (site discontinued).

Cross, Terry. 2002. "Spirituality and Mental Health: A Native American Perspective." *Focal Point* 16 (1): 22–24. http://pathwaysrtc.pdx.edu/pdf/fps0211.pdf.

Davis, Angela. 2003. *Are Prisons Obsolete?* New York: Seven Stories Press.

Davis-Young, Katherine. 2019. "For Many Native Americans, Embracing LGBT Members Is a Return to the Past." *Washington Post*, March 29, 2019.

DeHart, Dana. 2008. "Pathways to Prison: Impact of Victimization in the Lives of Incarcerated Women." *Violence against Women* 14 (12): 1362–81.

Deloria, Vine, Jr. 1969. *Custer Died for Your Sins: An Indian Manifesto*. New York: Macmillan.

———. 1994. *God Is Red: A Native View of Religion*. Golden CO: Fulcrum Publishing.

———. 1999. *Spirit and Reason: The Vine Deloria Jr. Reader*. Edited by B. Deloria, K. Foehner, and S. Scinta. Golden CO: Fulcrum Publishing.

————. 2006. *The World We Used to Live In: Remembering the Powers of the Medicine Men*. Golden CO: Fulcrum Publishing.

Dempsey, Hugh Aylmer. 1984. *Big Bear: The End of Freedom*. Vancouver BC: Douglas and McIntyre.

Dumond, Robert W. 2000. "Inmate Sexual Assaults: The Plague that Persists." *Prison Journal* 80 (4): 407–14. https://www.wcl.american.edu/endsilence/documents /InmateSexualAssaultThePlagueThatPersists.pdf.

Dunbar-Ortiz, Roxanne. 2014. *An Indigenous Peoples' History of the United States*. Boston: Beacon Press.

Duran, Eduardo. 2006. *Healing the Soul Wound: Counseling with American Indians and Other Native Peoples*. New York: Teachers College Press.

Duran, Eduardo, and Bonnie Duran. 1995. *Native American Postcolonial Psychology*. Albany: State University of New York Press.

Dusenberry, Verne. 1998. *The Montana Cree: A Study in Religious Persistence*. Norman: University of Oklahoma Press.

Fitzgerald, Judith, and Michael Oren Fitzgerald, eds. 2005. *The Spirit of Indian Women*. Bloomington IN: World Wisdom.

Fordham, Monique. 1993. "Within the Iron Houses: The Struggle for Native American Religious Freedom in American Prisons." *Social Justice* 20 (51–52): 165–71.

Foucault, Michel. (1975) 1977. *Discipline and Punish: The Birth of the Prison*. Translated by A. Sheridan. New York: Random House.

————. 1980. *Power/Knowledge: Selected Interviews and Other Writings, 1972–1977*. Edited by C. Gordon. New York: Random House.

Frampton, Mary Louise. 2019. "Doing Justice: An Interview with Abby Abinanti, Chief Judge of the Yurok Tribe (Part 1)." *Capitol Weekly*, June 21, 2019. https:// lostcoastoutpost.com/2019/jun/21/doing-justice-oral-history-abby-abinanti -chief-jud/.

Gentle Action. n.d. Accessed September 29, 2016. http://www.gentleaction.org (site discontinued).

Gikinoo'amaage, Nicola Mino. n.d. "Sweat Lodge Understanding." *Many Good Teachings* (blog). Accessed December 28, 2020. http://www.manygoodteachings.com /sweatlodge-understanding.html.

Glare, Aja. 2018. "On Special Assignment: Sexual Assault at Montana Women's Prison." *MTN News*, February 8, 2018.

Grant, Duane. 2019. Interview with the author, June 2019.

"Group Post: American Indians/Alaskan Natives." https://wp.vcu.edu/swog2015 /2016/03/02/group-post-american-indiansalaskan-natives/ (site discontinued).

Harmon, Amy. 2010. "Indian Tribe Was Right to Limit Research of Its DNA." *New York Times*, April 21, 2010. http://www.nytimes.com/2010/04/22/us/22dna .html?pagewanted=all&_r=1.

Hartney, C. 2008. *Native American Youth and the Juvenile Justice System*. March 2008. http://www.policyarchive.org/handle/10207/5712.

Harvey McCue and Associates. 2010. "Activities: 1. Coast Salish Story—Crow and Little Bear." In *The Learning Circle: Classroom Activities on First Nations of Canada* (Unit 3). Ottawa ON: Minister of Public Works and Government Services Canada. https://www.rcaanc-cirnac.gc.ca/eng/1316530132377/1535460393645#chpm3.

Heavy Runner, Iris, and Joann Sebastian Morris. 1997. "Traditional Native Culture and Resilience." *Spring 1997 Newsletter: Resiliency—A Paradigm Shift for Schools* 5 (1): 1–6. http://conservancy.umn.edu/bitstream/handle/11299/145989/TraditionalNativeCulture-and-Resilience.pdf?sequence=1&isAllowed=y.

Hendrix, Levanne R. 2017. "1953 to 1969: Policy of Termination and Relocation." Stanford School of Medicine: Ethnogeriatrics. https://geriatrics.stanford.edu/ethnomed/american_indian/learning_activities/learning_1/termination_relocation.html.

Hopper, Frank. 2020. "Potlatch in Prison: Tribal Sons." *Last Real Indians*, January 31, 2020. https://lastrealindians.com/news/2020/1/30/potlatch-in-prison-tribal-sons-by-frank-hopper.

Indian Child Welfare Act, 25 U.S.C. §§ 1901–63 (1978). http://dot.ca.gov/hq/tpp/offices/ocp/nalb/Images/Child_Indian_Welfare_Act.pdf.

Jenkins, A. 2016. "Washington Prisons to Cease Calling Inmates 'Offenders.'" Oregon Public Broadcasting, November 3, 2016.

Jurist. 2014. "Female Inmates and Sexual Assault." *Jurist*, September 15, 2014.

Kamenetz, Anya. 2017. "How to Apply the Brain Science of Resilience to the Classroom." National Public Radio, June 12, 2017. https://www.npr.org/sections/ed/2017/06/12/530893427/how-to-apply-the-brain-science-of-resilience-to-the-classroom.

Kirkup, Kristy, and Michael MacDonald. 2019. "'Predator' Prison Guard Accused of Sexually Assaulting 3 Women." *Canadian Press*, May 23, 2019. https://www.cbc.ca/news/canada/nova-scotia/prison-guard-sexual-assault-nova-scotia-1.5146248.

Kovach, Margaret. 2009. *Indigenous Methodologies: Characteristics, Conversations, and Contexts*. Toronto ON: University of Toronto Press.

LaDuke, Winona. 2005. *Recovering the Sacred: The Power of Naming and Claiming*. Cambridge MA: South End Press.

Lee, Mary. 2006. "Cree (Nehiyawak) Teaching" (lecture transcript). http://fourdirectionsteachings.com/transcripts/cree.pdf.

Lungren, Sam. 2012. "Rocky Boy's—Paid on the Plains." *Native News Project*, 2012. https://nativenews.jour.umt.edu/2012/stories/rocky-boys/.

Mandhane, Renu. 2020. "'Child Welfare to Prison Pipeline' Feeding Rising Indigenous Incarceration Rates." *Nation to Nation* (news show), January 23, 2020.

Maracle, Lee. 1996. *I Am Woman: A Native Perspective on Sociology and Feminism.* Vancouver BC: Press Gang Publishers.

McLeod, Neal. 2007. *Cree Narrative Memory: From Treaties to Contemporary Times.* Saskatoon SK: Purich Publishing.

MDOC (Montana Department of Corrections). 2015. *2015 Biennial Report to the People of Montana.* Deer Lodge: Montana Correctional Enterprise. http://cor.mt.gov /Portals/104/Resources/Reports/2015biennialReport.pdf, https://leg.mt.gov/content/Committees/Interim/2015-2016/Sentencing/Committee -Topics/Study-Resources/2015-corrections-biennial-report.pdf.

Mello, Michelle M., and Leslie E. Wolf. 2010. "The American Indian Tribe Case: Lessons for Research Involving Stored Biologic Samples." *New England Journal of Medicine* 363: 204–7. doi:10.1056/NEJMp1005203.

Meredith, H. 2016. "American Indians/Alaskan Natives" (group post, blog forum), March 2, 2016. https://wp.vcu.edu/swog2015/2016/03/02/group-post-american -indiansalaskan-natives/ (site discontinued).

Miller, Robert J. 2006. *Native America, Discovered and Conquered: Thomas Jefferson, Lewis & Clark, and Manifest Destiny.* Westport CT: Prager Publishers.

Mirsky, Laura. 2004. "Restorative Justice Practices of Native American, First Nation, and Other Indigenous People of North America: Part One." International Institute for Restorative Practices, April 27, 2004. https://www.iirp.edu/news/restorative -justice-practices-of-native-american-first-nation-and-other-indigenous-people -of-north-america-part-one.

Mochama, Vicky. 2018. "Treatment of Women in Canadian Prisons a Human Rights Travesty." *Toronto Star*, January 4, 2018.

Monture, Patricia A. 2009. "Women and Risk: Aboriginal Women, Colonialism, and Correctional Practice." In *First Voices: An Aboriginal Women's Reader*, edited by Patricia Monture and Patricia McGuire. Toronto ON: Inanna Publications.

Monture, Patricia, and Patricia McGuire, eds. 2009. *First Voices: An Aboriginal Women's Reader.* Toronto ON: Inanna Publications.

Moore, Kathleen Dean, Kurt Peters, Ted Jojola, and Amber Lacy, eds. 2007. *How It Is: The Native American Philosophy of V. F. Cordova.* Tucson: University of Arizona Press.

MWP (Montana Women's Prison). 2022. https://prisoninsight.com/correctional -facilities/state/montana/montana-womens-prison/.

NAMI (National Alliance on Mental Illness). 2003. "NAMI and American Indian & Alaska Native Leaders Meet to Build Partnerships and Alliances" (press release). June 29, 2003. https://www.nami.org/Press-Media/Press-Releases/2003/nami -and-American-Indian-Alaska-Native-Leaders-M.

National Center on Domestic and Sexual Violence. 2017. "Publications." http://www .ncdsv.org/publications_wheel.html.

National Institute of Justice. 2016. "Five Things about Violence against American Indian and Alaska Native Women and Men." November 30, 2016. https://nij .ojp.gov/topics/articles/five-things-about-violence-against-american-indian -and-alaska-native-women-and-men#two.

Native Science. n.d. "What Is Traditional Knowledge?" http://www.nativescience .org/html/traditional_knowledge.html.

Newcomb, Steven T. 2008. *Pagans in the Promised Land: Decoding the Doctrine of Christian Discovery.* Golden CO: Fulcrum Press.

Niezen, Ronald. 2000. *Spirit Wars: Native North American Religions in the Age of Nation Building.* Los Angeles: University of California Press.

Northwest Portland Area Indian Health Board. 2012. *Northwest American Indian and Alaska Native Mortality: A Summary of Death Certificate Data from Idaho, Oregon, and Washington.* Portland OR: Northwest Tribal EpiCenter. http://www.npaihb .org/images/epicenter_docs/nw-Idea/2012/nov2012/NativeMortalityReport _email.pdf.

ODOC (Oregon Department of Corrections). 2015. *Inmate Population Profile for 03/01/2015* (data file). https://www.oregon.gov/doc/resrch/docs/inmate_profile _201503.pdf.

———. 2022. "About Us." https://www.oregon.gov/doc/about/pages/prison-locations .aspx.

Onion, Rebecca. 2015. "The Pen." *Slate*, March 22, 2015. http://www.slate.com/articles /news_and_politics/history/2015/03/indiana_women_s_prison_a_revisionist _history.html.

Ono, Azusa. 2004. "The Relocation and Employment Assistance Programs, 1948–1970: Federal Indian Policy and the Early Development of the Denver Indian Community." *Indigenous Nations Studies Journal* 5 (1): 27–50. https://kuscholarworks .ku.edu/bitstream/handle/1808/5808/ins.v05.n1.27-50.pdf?sequence=1.

Pari Center. 2022 "F. David Peat." https://paricenter.com/f-david-peat/.

Partnership with Native Americans. 2022. "History and Culture: Termination Policy, 1953–68." http://www.nativepartnership.org/site/PageServer?pagename =pwna_Native_History_terminationpolicynp.

Peat, F. David. 2005. *Blackfoot Physics: A Journey into the Native American Worldview.* Newburyport MA: Weiser Books.

———. 2008. *Gentle Action: Bringing Creative Change to a Turbulent World.* Pari, Italy: Pari Publishing.

———. 2022. "Bibliography." http://www.fdavidpeat.com/bibliography/books /blackfoot.htm.

———. n.d. *Blackfoot Physics: A Journey into the Native American Universe.* F. David Peat.com. Accessed December 15, 2020. http://www.fdavidpeat.com /bibliography/books/blackfoot.htm.

Piecora, Christina. 2014. "Female Inmates and Sexual Assault." *Jurist*, September 15, 2014. http://www.jurist.org/dateline/2014/09/christina-piecora-female-inmates.php.

"Prison Insight." n.d. https://prisoninsight.com/correctional-facilities/state/montana/montana-womens-prison/.

Prison Legal News. 2013. "More Oregon Prison Employees Accused of Sexual Assault." *Prison Legal News*, April 15, 2013. https://www.prisonlegalnews.org/news/2013/apr/15/more-oregon-prison-employees-accused-of-sexual-abuse/.

Pullin, Zachary (Chippewa Cree). 2016. "Two Spirit: The Story of a Movement Unfolds" (blog). *Diverse Elders Coalition*, March 24, 2016.

RAINN. n.d. "Victims of Sexual Violence: Statistics." https://www.rainn.org/statistics/victims-sexual-violence.

Red Lodge Transition Services. n.d. "About: Incarceration Rates." Accessed December 28, 2020. http://redlodgetransition.org/about/.

Reinventing Reentry. 2020. "Reentry Simulations." https://www.reinventingreentry.org/reentry-simulation.html.

Rivas, Jorge. 2015. "The Number of Native Americans in Federal Prison Has Jumped 27 Percent in Five Years." Fusion—Injustice. April 21, 2015. http://fusion.net/story/123693/feds-reviewing-native-american-sentencing-disparities-again/.

Rocky Mountain Tribal Epidemiology Center. 2010. *Annual Report 2009–2010*. December 2010. Billings MT: RMTEC. http://www.rmtec.org/wp-content/uploads/2014/07/Annual-Report-2009-2010.pdf (site discontinued).

Ross, Luana. 1998. *Inventing the Savage: The Social Construction of Native American Criminality*. Austin: University of Texas Press.

Russell, Kirstin. 2016. Interview on contemporary judicial system, Rocky Boy's Indian Reservation. December 11, 2016.

Seven Dancers Coalition. 2019. "Restoring Harmony within Indigenous Communities." http://www.sevendancerscoalition.com/.

Smith, Linda Tuhiwai. 1999. *Decolonizing Methodologies: Research and Indigenous Peoples*. New York: St. Martin's Press.

Spence, Clark C. 1975. *Territorial Politics and Government in Montana, 1864–89*. Urbana: University of Illinois Press.

Stamper, Ed, Helen Windy Boy, and Ken Morsette. 2015. *The History of the Chippewa Cree of Rocky Boy's Indian Reservation*. Box Elder MT: Stone Child College.

Stanford Medicine. 2019. "1953 to 1969: Policy of Termination and Relocation." https://geriatrics.stanford.edu/ethnomed/american_indian/learning_activities/learning_1/termination_relocation.html.

Statista. 2022. "Child Abuse Rate in the United States in 2020, by Race/Ethnicity of the Victim." January 26, 2022. https://www.statista.com/statistics/254857/child-abuse-rate-in-the-us-by-race-ethnicity/.

Subia Big Foot, Delores. 2009. Statement. Seventh Generation Promise: Indian Youth Suicide Prevention Act, S. 1635, Hearing before the Committee on Indian Affairs, Senate. 111th Cong.

Sullivan, Harry. 2019. "Three Inmates at Women's Prison in Truro Accuse Guard of Sex Assaults." *Truro Daily*, May 23, 2019.

SUNY Oneonta. n.d. Philosophy. https://suny.oneonta.edu/philosophy/majors-programs.

Ten Fingers, Tony. 2014. *Lakota Wisdom*. Colorado Springs: Alpine Line Publications.

Thackeray, Lorna. 2011. "Reasons for Suicide Amplified for Native Americans." *Billings Gazette*, February 20, 2011.

ThoughtCo. 2017. "Sociology." https://www.thoughtco.com/sociology-4133515.

Tribal Access to Justice Innovation. 2022. "Muscogee Creek Reintegration Program." https://tribaljustice.org/places/corrections-reentry/muscogee-creek-reintegration-program/.

———. n.d. "The Port Gamble S'Klallam Re-Entry Program." https://tribaljustice.org/places/specialized-court-projects/re-entry-program/.

Trombley, Harlan. 2015. "Trombley Tapped to Represent Corrections on New Initiatives." *American Indian Liaison Bulletin*, October 5, 2015. https://cor.mt.gov/Publications/Media/american-indian-liaison-bulletin-trombley-tapped-to-represent-corrections-on-new-initiatives.

Tyner, Artika R. 2021. "Ending the School to Prison Pipeline" (blog post and keynote). January 23, 2021. https://www.artikatyner.com/new-blog/2021/1/23/ending-the-school-to-prison-pipeline.

Uken, Cindy. 2013. "Montana Tribes Seek Solutions to Reducing Suicides." *Missoulian*, April 7, 2013.

U.S. Department of Justice, Office of Justice Programs. 2010. *Parents in Prison and Their Minor Children* (NCJ 222984). March 2010. http://www.bjs.gov/content/pub/pdf/pptmc.pdf.

Vera. n.d. "17 States Open up Prisons and Jails to Local Communities—and National Leaders—to Foster Transparency as Part of National Prison Visiting Week." https://www.vera.org/newsroom/17-states-open-up-prisons-and-jails-local-communities-national-prison-visiting-week.

Viveros, Miguel. 2020. "Previously Incarcerated Students Form Re-Entry Club at Clark College." *Indy: Clark College's Student Run News Publication*, March 14, 2020. https://clarkindy.com/2020/03/14/previously-incarcerated-students-form-re-entry-club-at-clark-college/.

Wagner, Peter. 2004. "Importing Constituents: Prisoners and Political Clout in Montana." *Prison Policy Initiative*. December 14, 2004. http://www.prisonersofthecensus.org/montana/importing.html.

Wenger-Nabigon, Annie. 2010. "The Cree Medicine Wheel as Organizing Paradigm of Theories of Human Development." *Native Social Work Journal* 7: 139–61. https://zone.biblio.laurentian.ca/bitstream/10219/387/1/nswj-v7-art6-p139-161.pdf.

Whitford, Judge Melody. 2016. Interview on contemporary judicial system, Rocky Boy's Indian Reservation. December 11, 2016.

Wiebe, Rudy. 2008. *Extraordinary Canadians: Big Bear*. Edited by J. R. Saul. Toronto ON: Penguin Group.

Williams, Steven Lyn. 2012. "Smudging the Book: The Role of Cultural Authority in Tribal Historical Narratives and Revitalization at Rocky Boy." PhD diss., University of Iowa. http://ir.uiowa.edu/etd/3405/.

Wiltz, Teresa. 2016. "American Indian Girls Often Fall through the Cracks." *Pew Charitable Trusts: Stateline*. March 4, 2016. http://www.pewtrusts.org/en/research-and-analysis/blogs/stateline/2016/03/04/american-indian-girls-often-fall-through-the-cracks.

Woodworth, Whitney. 2020. "Sex, Lies and Cellphones: Reports of Misconduct at Coffee Creek Women's Prison Persist." *Salem Statesman Journal,* January 21, 2020.

Zapata, Karina. 2020. "Decolonizing Mental Health: The Importance of an Oppression-Focused Mental Health System." *Calgary Journal,* February 27, 2020. https://calgaryjournal.ca/more/calgaryvoices/4982-decolonizing-mental-health-the-importance-of-an-oppression-focused-mental-health-system.html/.

INDEX

Cooper, Arnold, 146

Correctional Service of Canada (CSC), 28–33

Corrections and Conditional Release Act, 29

counseling, within Montana Women's Prison (MWP), 52–53

creative suspension, 93, 130

Cree Nation. *See* Chippewa Cree Nation

criminality, 48, 132, 133

Cross, Terry, 69

Crow and Little Bear legend, 99–105

culture/Native culture, 50–51, 61–62, 66, 86

Custer Died for Your Sins (Deloria), 35

custodial sexual abuse law, 14

Davis, Angela, 47

Davis-Young, Katherine, 57

decolonization, 67–68

DeHart, Dana, 20

Deloria, Vine, Jr., 35, 36, 37, 38–39

Dempsey, Hugh, 37

Denny, George, 23, 61–62, 137

depression, 68

detention center, at Rocky Boy's Indian Reservation, 115

Diabetes Project, 97–99

discipline, 44–45, 62

Discipline and Punish (Foucault), 41–45

disease, 9

distrust, by Native Americans, 72

Diyin Dine'é (Holy People), 140–42

Domestic Abuse Intervention Project, 24

domesticity, within women's prisons, 47–48

Donald E. Long Juvenile Detention Facility, 16

driving while intoxicated (DWI), 1

drugs/drug abuse: incarceration regarding, 49; following Indian Relocation Act, 36; mental health and, 72; personal story regarding, 18, 70; within prisons, 14; following prison sentence, 51; sexual favors and, 60; as survival strategy, 20

Dumond, Robert, 60

Dunbar-Ortiz, Roxanne, 39

Duran, Bonnie, 75

Duran, Eduardo, 66–67, 75

Earl E. Bakken Center for Spirituality and Healing (University of Minnesota), 105

education, 19, 51–52

Elders: approaching, 86; healing viewpoint of, 114; hope through, 89; personal story regarding, 87; within reintegration program, 30–31; role of, 61–62, 114–15

Elders Panel, at Rocky Boy's Indian Reservation, 117

Elizabeth Fry Society, 15

emotional healing, 71. *See also* healing; mental health

epistemological hybridism, 66–67

escorted temporary absences (ETA), 30

excuse-making, as societal reaction, 133

execution, 41–42

extended family, Native American culture regarding, 61–62, 78

extradition, 2

family culture, of Native Americans, 61–62

family history, as influencing factor, 20

family reunification, programs regarding, 26

felons, 44, 145–46

First Foods Feast, 59, 120, 123
First Nations, 21, 28–33, 83–85, 115, 135–36
First Nations Cree of Canada, 118
First Voices (Monture), 114
flexibility, 107, 127, 136–37
Fond du Lac Band of Lake Superior Chippewa, 19
food, conditions of, 12–13
Forum on Corrections Research, 31
foster care system, 16
Foucault, Michel, 41–45
FourDirectionsTeachings.com, 77–80
Fowler, Marilyn, 95–96
Fried, Stanley, 38

Galanda, Gabe, 143
Gandhi, Mahatma, 106
gangs, 16, 18
garden project, within Montana Women's Prison (MWP), 26
gender, Native American viewpoint regarding, 57–58
general public, reentry and, 144–45
generational trauma, 68–69. *See also* trauma
gentle action theory: Chippewa Cree Nation and, 99–105; context and, 133; creative suspension within, 93, 130; Crow and Little Bear legend as, 99–105; defined, 92–93; delivery method of, 109; Diabetes Project and, 97–99; facets of, 93; flexibility and, 127, 136–37; gentle action within, 93–96; good motives within, 136; harmony and, 137; within Healing the Sacred Hoop workshop, 105, 108–9, 138; Indo-International School (India) and,

94–95; metaphor regarding, 94; objective of, 93; overview of, 6, 66, 106–7, 136–37; purpose of, 134; reflections on, 126–34; relationship within, 137; relevance of, for Indian country, 96–99; respect within, 136; social organism within, 94; timing for, 130; of traditional justice, 118; as transformative, 137; trust within, 94, 137
gifting, 86, 87, 104–5, 146
Goare, Aja, 14
God Is Red (Deloria), 37
gold, discovery of, 8, 9
Grant, Duane, 37–38
Grant, Ulysses S., 8–9
green dot identification, 16–17
grief, 65, 67, 86–87

Hall, Brandy, 56
Halpern, Emma, 15
Hansen, Jeannie, 14
harmony, gentle action theory and, 137
Harris, Nadine, 21–22
hatred, trauma and, 85–86
Havasupai Tribe, 97–99
healing: of deep-soul wounds, 66; Elder viewpoint regarding, 114; emotional, 71; of grief, 86–87; harmony through, 67; identity and, 153; importance of, 89; Medicine Wheel and, 77–80; Native American worldview and, 75–76; need for ceremonies of, 85–86; purpose of, 134; ritual and ceremony as part of, 70, 71, 120; Rocky Boy's Indian Reservation ceremonies for, 86–89; smudging and, 83–85; sweat lodge and, 80–83; traditional practices

In the New Visions in Native American and Indigenous Studies series

Ojibwe Stories from the Upper Berens River: A. Irving Hallowell and Adam Bigmouth in Conversation
Edited and with an introduction by Jennifer S. H. Brown

The Incarceration of Native American Women: Creating Pathways to Wellness and Recovery through Gentle Action Theory
Carma Corcoran

Ute Land Religion in the American West, 1879–2009
Brandi Denison

Blood Will Tell: Native Americans and Assimilation Policy
Katherine Ellinghaus

Ecology and Ethnogenesis: An Environmental History of the Wind River Shoshones, 1000–1868
Adam R. Hodge

Of One Mind and Of One Government: The Rise and Fall of the Creek Nation in the Early Republic
Kevin Kokomoor

Invisible Reality: Storytellers, Storytakers, and the Supernatural World of the Blackfeet
Rosalyn R. LaPier

Indigenous Languages and the Promise of Archives
Edited by Adrianna Link, Abigail Shelton, and Patrick Spero

Life of the Indigenous Mind: Vine Deloria Jr. and the Birth of the Red Power Movement
David Martínez

Everywhen: Australia and the Language of Deep History
Ann McGrath, Laura Rademaker, and Jakelin Troy

All My Relatives: Exploring Lakota Ontology, Belief, and Ritual
David C. Posthumus

Standing Up to Colonial Power: The Lives of Henry Roe and Elizabeth Bender Cloud
Renya K. Ramirez

Walking to Magdalena: Personhood and Place in Tohono O'odham Songs, Sticks, and Stories
Seth Schermerhorn

To order or obtain more information on these or other University of Nebraska Press titles, visit nebraskapress.unl.edu.